"THE SADDEST SHIP AFLOAT"
The Tragedy of the MS *St. Louis*

Allison Lawlor

NIMBUS
PUBLISHING LTD

Nimbus Publishing Limited
3731 Mackintosh St, Halifax, NS, B3K 5A5
(902) 455-4286 nimbus.ca

Printed and bound in Canada

NB1172

Cover and interior design: Jenn Embree
Cover photo: United States Holocaust Memorial Museum (top)
Art Resource New York (bottom)

Library and Archives Canada Cataloguing in Publication

Lawlor, Allison, 1971-, author
"The saddest ship afloat" : the tragedy of the MS St. Louis / Allison Lawlor.
Includes bibliographical references and index.
ISBN 978-1-77108-399-7 (paperback)

1. St. Louis (Ship). 2. Jewish refugees—History—20th century. 3. Jews—
Germany—History—20th century. 4. Holocaust, Jewish (1939-1945). 5.
Canada—Emigration and immigration—Government policy. I. Title.

DS134.255.L39 2016   940.53'18   C2015-908198-X

Nimbus Publishing acknowledges the financial support for its publishing activi-
ties from the Government of Canada through the Canada Book Fund (CBF)
and the Canada Council for the Arts, and from the Province of Nova Scotia.
We are pleased to work in partnership with the Province of Nova Scotia to
develop and promote our creative industries for the benefit of all Nova Scotians.

CONTENTS

The MS *St. Louis* sails out of Hamburg, Germany, in front of cheering crowds of Nazi soldiers. COURTESY OF ART RESOURCE NEW YORK

PREFACE

LONG BEFORE THE SHIP MADE headlines around the world in the spring of 1939, the MS (motor ship) *St. Louis* was a familiar sight in Halifax. The German transatlantic liner made the city a regular port of call during the 1930s.

Built by the Bremer Vulkan shipyards in Bremen, Germany, for the Hamburg-America Line, the *St. Louis* was a diesel-powered ship 175 metres long—about the equivalent length of two soccer fields. Named after King Louis IX of France, the ship could carry 973 passengers.

The *St. Louis* regularly sailed from Hamburg to Halifax and New York, which, in the 1930s, was dubbed Luxury Liner Row. Ten Atlantic liners could be docked in the American port in one day. Built for both transatlantic liner service and for leisure cruises, the *St. Louis* made cruises all the way to the West Indies.

Considered a medium-sized liner, the *St. Louis* operated during an age of splendour for cruising. The 1930s was the peak for the transatlantic liners. Considered by many to be a frivolous endeavour, transatlantic cruising consisted of making a series of calls to exotic ports and ended with a return to the port of origin. During the cruise, passengers were entertained onboard with fine food, music, and dancing. The 1930s was the ultimate age for luxury, size, splendour, even fantasy for the great liners, according to William Miller, the author of several books on ocean liners and cruise ships.

A REGULAR PORT OF CALL

The *St. Louis*'s maiden voyage to Halifax was in 1929 and came at a critical time in the port's history. Halifax was bustling. In 1928, Halifax Harbour was considered the second-largest natural harbour in the world, surpassed only by Sydney, Australia. It was a port of call for "most of the large cabin class passenger vessels enroute from Europe to New York," according to a February 1929 brief from the Halifax Harbour Commission. It was considered the Canadian port for regular cargo and passenger service, as well as coastal services for passenger and freight.

HAMBURG-AMERIKA LINIE

(Compañía Hamburguesa Americana)

No. 2033

Touristenklasse
Clase Turista
Tourist Class

Motorschiff motonave motor vessel } St. Louis

am d salir sailing } 13. Mai 1939

von de from } Hamburg

nach á to } Havana

Name des Reisenden:
nombre del pasajero:
passenger's name:

Herr Dr. Walter

Weissler

Bezahlter Fahrpreis
Pasaje pagado — Fare paid

Boarding pass of *St. Louis* passenger Walter Weissler.

In 1928, the city had completed an ocean terminals project that was critical in attracting ocean liners. The project offered large piers with full railway access, refrigerated storage, grain elevators, and an integrated train station, hotel, and immigration terminal at Pier 21. The additions allowed liners to quickly and easily dock and let passengers off. The long stretch of Piers 20, 21, and 22 could even dock two of the biggest liners in the world at the same time.

Halifax became an attractive port for small and medium-sized liners like the *St. Louis*, or the Cunard Line's *Ascania*, which visited the city more

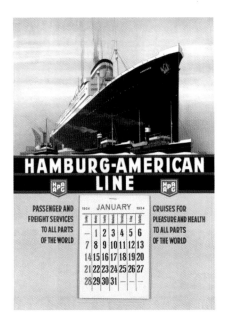

German graphic artist Ottomar Anton created promotional posters for many shipping companies, like this one advertising the Hamburg-America Line, **c. 1930.** COURTESY OF THE MARITIME MUSEUM OF THE ATLANTIC

than two hundred times. Halifax was often an intermediate port where the liners would stop to let off Canadian passengers and immigrants before continuing on to larger ports like New York.

The *St. Louis* called on Halifax at least two dozen times. During this period, the Halifax port had forty-eight shipping lines using its facilities, and as many as 1,600 steamers used the port in 1929. There were other ships that regularly called on Halifax including the *Kungsholm* of the Swedish-American Line and the *Minnewaska* of American Transport Lines.

The *St. Louis*'s last recorded visit to the Halifax port was in April 1939, just one month before it set off for Havana on its infamous voyage with more than nine hundred Jewish refugees onboard.

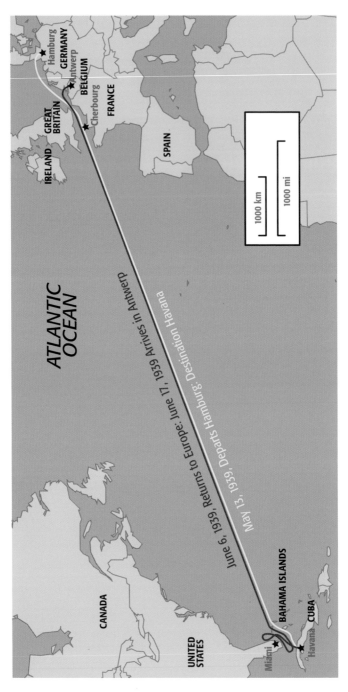

The MS *St. Louis* left Hamburg, Germany, on May 13, 1939, destined for Havana, Cuba. On June 6, the ship was forced to turn back to Europe. On June 17, the *St. Louis* landed in Antwerp, Belgium, after more than a month at sea.

INTRODUCTION

"As human beings we should do our best to provide as much sanctuary as we can for those people who can get away. I say we should do that because these people are human and deserve that consideration, and because we are human and ought to act in that way."

—MP Stanley Knowles, in the House of Commons on July 9, 1943

In the spring of 1939 Canada had a difficult choice to make. The MS *St. Louis*, a German luxury ship carrying hundreds of scared and persecuted Jewish refugees, was sailing in the Atlantic Ocean, just two days away from the port of Halifax. It was moving farther out to sea, having just sailed close to the Florida shore hoping to land. Denied a safe haven first by Cuba and then by the United States, Halifax remained one of the last possible ports of asylum in North America for the Jewish passengers, who feared they would be killed if they returned home to Nazi Germany. Potentially so close to safety off the coast of North America, in the end they were tragically far away.

After reading headlines like "Refugee Ship Idles off Florida Coast" on the front page of the *New York Times* and "Coast Guard Trails Tragic Liner as it Wanders Aimlessly in Florida Waters" in the *Washington Post*, some Canadians began to worry about the Jewish refugees onboard the MS *St. Louis*. A small group of Canadians made valiant efforts to provide sanctuary for the more than nine hundred Jewish refugees onboard the ship. Unfortunately, indifferent and anti-Semitic government officials in Ottawa refused appeals to let the ship dock. Had Prime Minister William Lyon Mackenzie King's government

SECOND WORLD WAR TERMINOLOGY

The *Nazi Party*, which came to power in Germany in January 1933, believed Germans were racially superior and Jews were an inferior group that threatened the German community. Adolf Hitler, leader of the party, believed (among other things) Jews had devised a conspiracy which caused Germany to lose the First World War, and that Jews had specifically designed the 1919 Treaty of Versailles to bring Germany down.

The Nazis promoted *anti-Semitism*: prejudice against, or hatred of, Jewish people. Those who promoted anti-Semitism were called anti-Semites. This attitude resulted in unkind portrayals of Jews in propaganda posters and newspaper ads.

Anti-Semitism led to the *Holocaust*, the state-sponsored persecution and murder of six million Jewish people by the Nazis and their collaborators. Holocaust is a Greek word meaning "sacrifice by fire."

The Holocaust led to a crisis of Jewish *refugees* in Europe. A refugee is a person who is forced to leave their country of citizenship because of persecution based on race, religion, nationality, culture, or political belief. He or she cannot return home for fear of continued persecution.

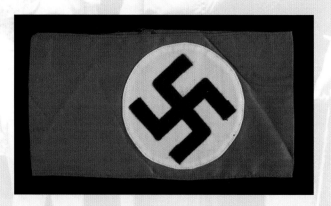

Members of the Nazi Party wore these red armbands emblazoned with a swastika over their uniforms. COURTESY OF THE UNITED STATES HOLOCAUST MEMORIAL MUSEUM

decided differently, the *St. Louis* would likely have been welcomed at Pier 21 in Halifax.

Captain Gustav Schröder had no choice but to sail back to Europe. Ultimately, 254 of his 937 passengers died in concentration camps. Entire families and children as young as six were among those killed. *The New York Times* would dub it "the saddest ship afloat."

The turning away of the MS *St. Louis* became a powerful symbol of not only Canada's, but the world's, apathy and indifference to the troubles facing European Jews on the eve of the Second World War.

When Adolf Hitler rose to power, becoming chancellor of Germany in 1933, the country was suffering from economic collapse, and part of his solution was to make Jewish citizens the scapegoats. Getting rid of them, he said, would solve the country's problems. Jews throughout Germany increasingly feared for their lives. As the head of the German government, he passed more and more anti-Semitic laws and by 1939, every Jewish person had to self-identify with a yellow badge. These badges were shaped like the Star of David, an important Jewish symbol, and emblazoned with "Jude," the German word for "Jew." This was so Nazis and

One of the yellow Star of David badges European Jews were forced to wear during the Second World War. COURTESY OF THE UNITED STATES HOLOCAUST MEMORIAL MUSEUM

The broken glass of Lichtenstein Leather Goods in Berlin, a Jewish-owned business that was destroyed during Kristallnacht. COURTESY OF THE UNITED STATES HOLOCAUST MEMORIAL MUSEUM

other anti-Semites could easily pick them out. The Nazi Party issued leaflets depicting the badges that read: *Wer dieses Zeichen trägt, ist ein Feind unseres Volkes | Whoever bears this sign is an enemy of our people.*

Huge numbers of Jewish families searched frantically for a place to go and many tried to leave Germany. But leaving was difficult: individuals needed visas and money to enter another country. And many countries, like Canada, were not eager to accept Jews fleeing Europe. They feared they would be overrun by a flood of refugees if they did.

On November 9, 1938, a horrible event now known as Kristallnacht (pronounced *crees-tall-not*), or "the night of broken glass," took place. Jewish-owned businesses in Nazi Germany and parts of Austria were looted and ransacked while hundreds of synagogues had their windows smashed and were set afire. Ninety-five people were murdered, and thirty thousand Jewish men were arrested and taken to concentration camps.

Canadians disapproved of the Nazis' brutality and their persecution of Jews and other minorities, but weren't willing to take meaningful action and open their country to the refugees. Anti-Semitism ran deep enough that many Canadians didn't want Jewish neighbours. Like Germany, Canada was facing tough economic times because of the impending war, and people feared "foreigners" would put too much pressure on the country's already limited resources.

With few passenger ships available to take them and few countries willing to accept them, only a small percentage of Jews made it out of Germany before the war started. They went to countries like Cuba, the United States, England, and Canada. While many Canadians asked Prime Minister William Lyon Mackenzie King to accept Jewish refugees fleeing Nazi Germany in the late 1930s and early 1940s, his government, like many others, refused. In fact, Canada had one of the worst records of all; during Hitler's reign, the country only granted permission for about five thousand Jews to enter.

Cuba was the only country close to the United States willing to accept refugees in large numbers, but acceptance usually came at a steep price. Sometimes, even after paying government officials large amounts of money, they were still denied entry.

When the MS *St. Louis* departed Hamburg in 1939, every passenger onboard had what he or she thought was a legal landing permit. It was only after the ship set sail that the pro-fascist Cuban government invalidated the certificates. Some Cuban politicians were greedy—after their government ruled that the certificates could not be used as visas, they pocketed the money refugees had

A postcard from the 1930s depicting the MS *St. Louis.* COURTESY OF THE UNITED STATES HOLOCAUST MEMORIAL MUSEUM

paid. Most of the *St. Louis*'s passengers had applied for United States visas in addition to their Cuban papers. They planned to stay in Cuba until the American Bureau of Immigration and Naturalization approved their visas and they could settle in the United States. In the end, the passengers aboard the *St. Louis* were denied entry into Cuba, a country that had promised them safety, and were forced to sail back to Europe before their American visa numbers ever came up. US visas were issued on a first-come, first-served basis, and applicants had to wait for their numbers to come up before they were allowed to enter the country. The wait could be anywhere from three months to three years. After Cuba, the United States, and Canada all refused them sanctuary, more than two hundred and fifty *St. Louis* passengers died in concentration camps in Nazi-occupied Europe.

Berechtigt zur Fahr-
preisermässigung
auf den Staatsbah-
nen gemäss den ta-
rifarischen Ermässi-
gungen für die
Schuljugend.

Uprawnia do ulgo-
wych przejazdów
kolejami państwo-
wemi według ulg
taryfowych dla mło-
dzieży szkolnej.

Unterschrift des Inhabers des Ausweises
podpis właściciela legitymacji

Gültig bis zum
30. September 19 16
Ważna do dnia
30 września 19 r.
Stempel der Schule
Pieczęć szkoły

Gültig bis zum
31 März 19
Ważna do dnia
31 marca 19
Stempel der Schule
Pieczęć szkoły

The stamped passport of Marianne Echt, who arrived in
Halifax through Pier 21 in 1939. COURTESY OF PIER 21 MUSEUM
OF IMMIGRATION

Some passengers who survived the war eventually immigrated
to the United States or to Canada to start new lives. Sol Messinger
was one of them. He was six years old when he and his family left
Germany in 1939 on the *St. Louis*. After the war, his family immigrated to the United States, where Sol ultimately became a doctor.

Marianne Echt knew she and her family were lucky to escape
Nazi Europe. Just months before Sol and the other passengers

Stanley Howard Knowles at his desk, c. 1942–48. Knowles was the parliamentary house leader for Canada's Co-operative Commonwealth Federation (CCF), later the New Democratic Party (NDP). LIBRARY AND ARCHIVES CANADA

aboard the MS *St. Louis* were told they could not enter Canada, the Echts arrived at Pier 21 in Halifax in March 1939, about to embark on a new life. The thirteen-year-old Jewish girl had fled with her family from the Free State of Danzig (now Gdańsk, Poland) on the steamship *Andania*. While so many others had been denied, Marianne and her family were one of the few Jewish families to find Canada's doors open on the eve of the Second World War.

Close to eighty years after the start of the Second World War, the story of the *St. Louis* and Canada's policy toward Jewish refugees provides us with a glimpse into a dark moment in Canadian history—a moment when the country could have provided a helping hand, but didn't. It is a story of war, prejudice, and the many other factors that continue to shape Canada's immigration policies.

After the war ended, Canada slowly started opening its doors to displaced people, including Jews. Canadians had seen the terrible effects of war and hatred, and softened their attitudes. Canada would eventually become one of the largest refugee-receiving countries in the world—something Canadians take pride in today.

In January 2011, a memorial to the MS *St. Louis* and its fateful voyage was unveiled at Pier 21 in Halifax—the place the ship would have docked had the government allowed it. The memorial evokes uncomfortable memories of a less tolerant time, but also serves as a necessary reminder to ensure similar situations never take place again.

A c. 1940 Nazi propaganda poster depicting Adolf Hitler; it reads "One people, one country, one leader!" COURTESY OF THE UNITED STATES HOLOCAUST MEMORIAL MUSEUM

CHAPTER 1

LIFE IN 1930s GERMANY

SOL MESSINGER WAS BORN IN Berlin, Germany, on June 16, 1932. He and his family had little idea of the dramatic course their lives would take during his first seven years. Six short months after Sol's birth, Adolf Hitler came to power. Being Jewish, the Messingers felt the anti-Semitism already present in Germany rising under Hitler's reign. Sol was less than a year old when the first of more than four hundred anti-Jewish laws and decrees were issued. As Sol got older, he and his family were excluded more and more from public life in their own country.

On September 15, 1935, the Nuremberg Laws were passed in Germany. Racial purity was decreed, which meant the Nazis believed Germans were members of a "master race," and were therefore superior physically and intellectually to all other people. The Nazis prevented Germans from mixing and being friends with "inferior" people, such as Jews. They encouraged "healthy" (German) members of society to have children, and discouraged everyone else from starting families. As a result, marriage between Germans and Jews was outlawed, and Jews had their citizenship revoked. Life for Jewish people became not only difficult, but downright dangerous.

Soon Jews were no longer allowed to hold jobs in the civil service, Jewish teachers were dismissed, caps were introduced on how many Jewish children could enter German schools, Jewish doctors' practices were restricted, and Jewish lawyers were disbarred.

A Nazi solider in front of the Jewish-owned Tietz Department Store with a boycott sign that reads: "Germans! Defend yourselves! Don't buy from Jews!" COURTESY OF THE UNITED STATES HOLOCAUST MEMORIAL MUSEUM

Sol's parents worried constantly about his safety. One day, as Sol watched from the family's apartment window, some Germans threw stones at the windows of a Jewish store across the street. They burst into the store through the broken windows and stole goods. "It was just a horrible feeling," he said in a 1991 interview that is part of the oral history collection at the United States Holocaust Memorial Museum in Washington, DC.

THE US HOLOCAUST MEMORIAL MUSEUM

The United States Holocaust Memorial Museum in Washington, DC, is a living memorial to the Holocaust. Its goal is to inspire people and governments around the world to study hatred in hope of preventing future genocides, a term which refers to violent crimes committed against groups of people with the intent to destroy the entire group. The museum also works to promote respect worldwide for each person's dignity and self-worth.

Since 1993, the museum has welcomed more than thirty-eight million visitors, including more than ten million children. The museum's website, the world's leading online authority on the Holocaust, is available in fifteen languages.

The museum has a permanent exhibit detailing the voyage of the *St. Louis*, which includes photographs, the ship's passenger list, and Captain Gustav Schröder's hat. It also has an extensive collection of interviews conducted with *St. Louis* passengers.

Outside the USHMM. COURTESY OF THE UNITED STATES HOLOCAUST MEMORIAL MUSEUM

FINDING A WAY OUT OF GERMANY

As Hitler passed more anti-Semitic laws, Sol's parents decided to leave the country for the family's safety. "It became clear that there was little if any future for Jews in Germany.... A lot of people began trying to find a way out of Germany," Sol recalled. But getting out of Germany wasn't easy for the Messingers or any other Jewish family in the late 1930s.

Sol's father was a tailor with a modest income. He saved every bit of money he could and applied for visas to the US. Like a passport, a visa is an official government document, and it gives permission for a person to enter a particular country. It was a difficult and expensive process and there was a long waiting list. The family was given a waiting number, which meant it might be several years before they could leave Germany. Several members of Sol's family, including two of his aunts, had already obtained visas.

Since it was difficult to gain entry to the United States directly, the Messingers decided to travel to Cuba where they would wait until they were allowed into the US. But before the family could get permits to Cuba, they faced more trouble at home.

Late one night in October 1938, Sol and his family were awoken by a loud knock on the door. It was the official secret police of Nazi Germany—the Gestapo. That night Sol's father was dragged away and deported to Poland, his birthplace.

After Sol's father was deported, life only got worse for the Messinger family. Less than a month after the visit from the Gestapo, a night of deadly attacks (later known as Kristallnacht— "the night of broken glass") took place throughout Nazi Germany and Austria. Paramilitary forces and non-Jewish civilians smashed the windows of Jewish-owned stores, and hundreds of synagogues were burned. Shards of broken glass littered the streets, and ninety-five people were murdered.

CONCENTRATION AND EXTERMINATION CAMPS

The first Nazi concentration camps were set up in Germany in March 1933, after Hitler became chancellor and his Nazi Party had control over the police. Nazi Germany established concentration and extermination camps throughout the territories it controlled, although there is sometimes confusion between the two kinds of camps.

Concentration camps were built before the war and early in Hitler's rule, and were not actually built to kill Jewish citizens. Some Jews were sent there, but so were Gypsies, Black people, and anyone who opposed the Nazi regime. Conditions inside concentration camps were appalling—abuse and starvation were common—but they were primarily built to intimidate the population into following Nazi law.

Extermination camps, on the other hand, were all built during the war and located in Nazi-occupied Poland. These camps had one purpose: to murder anyone who opposed Nazi rule. Most people who arrived at these camps were killed instantly in the large gas chambers.

Some of the confusion exists because the largest camp of all, Auschwitz, was both a concentration and extermination camp. It opened in 1940 and was an especially horrendous version of the prewar concentration camp, which eventually became an extermination camp. It is estimated that between 1940 and 1945, Auschwitz camp authorities murdered about 1.1 million men, women, and children.

A charcoal drawing created by David Friedmann based on his time in Auschwitz–Birkenau. Artist's caption: "Jewish prisoners on their way to bury a shot down comrade. A smiling and smoking Nazi is watching as two other prisoners are digging a grave. Usually, the prisoners dug their own graves before they were shot. This was an added enjoyment for the Nazis." COURTESY OF THE UNITED STATES HOLOCAUST MEMORIAL MUSEUM

GESTAPO AND NAZIS

The *Geheime Staatspolizei*—the German name for secret state police, which is usually shortened to "Gestapo"—was formally organized after the Nazi Party came to power in 1933. The Gestapo was responsible for rounding up Jews and other people the Nazis considered unfit for society and sending them to concentration camps.

The Nationalsozialistische Deutsche Arbeiterpartei (National Socialist German Workers' Party), usually just called the Nazi Party, was a political party in Germany, active between 1920 and 1945. Adolf Hitler became the party's leader in 1921.

Sol's parents knew then they had to get the family out of Germany as soon as possible. In April 1939, they received what they believed were the necessary entry visas for Cuba. They booked a passage on the Hamburg-America Line's motor ship the *St. Louis* and the day before they were set to meet the ship in the port of

The Hamburg-America Line motor ship *St. Louis* was built in by the German shipbuilding company Bremer Vulcan in 1928. COURTESY OF HERITAGE SHIPS

Hamburg, Sol's father returned from Poland on a temporary pass. Such passes were rarely issued, and he knew he was lucky to be reunited with his family.

The Messingers boarded the ship, hopeful they would find asylum and refuge in North America, blissfully unaware they would end up back where they started in little more than a month's time.

The MS *St. Louis* setting sail from the Port of Hamburg in 1939. COURTESY OF THE UNITED STATES HOLOCAUST MEMORIAL MUSEUM

As the MS *St. Louis* steamed out of Hamburg, a passenger looked back to snap this photograph from the ship's main deck. COURTESY OF THE UNITED STATES HOLOCAUST MEMORIAL MUSEUM

CHAPTER 2

ONBOARD THE
MS *ST. LOUIS*

ON MAY 13, 1939, a loud horn blasted, signalling the departure of the *St. Louis* from the harbour in Hamburg. Cheers erupted from the people lining the ship's decks. "My parents heaved a sigh of relief when the ship set sail," Sol remembered.

Music played and flags flew. There was excitement and relief among the passengers. Not only were they leaving Nazi Germany, but they were also embarking on a new adventure, moving to a new country, learning a new language, and for many, reuniting with family members who had left earlier. But along with the excitement was a sense of anxiety about the challenges they would face as immigrants in a new country, and a lot of sadness. They were leaving friends, family, and the country that had been their home—likely never to return.

Life onboard the *St. Louis* was luxurious. The eight-decked vessel of the Hamburg-America Line—which had previously sailed to Halifax on several passenger trips—had a swimming pool, fine dining, and plenty of live music. The ship had room for more than four hundred first-class passengers (who paid about $320 each for their tickets), and more than five hundred tourist-class passengers (who paid about $240 each per ticket). The cost of each passenger's ticket included a "contingency fee" of about $92 that was meant to protect the Hamburg-America Line against losses should the ship need to make an unplanned return voyage to Germany. But no one was thinking about that when the ship set sail in May.

The luxurious and spacious dining room offered fine dining three times a day.

Passengers enjoy a little fun in the sun in the ship's on-deck swimming pool.

CAPTAIN GUSTAV SCHRÖDER

The ship's captain, Gustav Schröder, was told to expect 899 Jewish passengers to board in Hamburg. His instructions were to stop in Cherbourg, France, to pick up 38 more. The total passenger count on the voyage from Europe to Cuba was 937. Only 6 of those passengers—a couple from Cuba and 4 people from Spain—were not Jewish.

Most of the passengers were carrying permits, which they believed would allow them to legally enter Cuba. Many of them had bought the expensive papers from Manuel Benitez Gonzalez, Cuba's director of immigration at the time. What they didn't know was much of that money had ended up in Benitez Gonzalez's own pocket and not with the government. He was re-ported to have illegally sold landing permits for $150 or more.

Of the 937 passengers onboard the MS *St. Louis*, 724 also had visas for the United States. But since there was a limit, or quota, on the number of Jews or other immigrants allowed into the United States, each visa had a quota number on it. The passengers planned to stay in Cuba while wait-ing for their US numbers to come up.

As they boarded the ship, passengers wrote their names in a log. COURTESY OF THE UNITED STATES HOLOCAUST MEMORIAL MUSEUM

Captain Schröder, a thirty-seven-year veteran of the Hamburg-America Line, instructed the 231 members of his crew that the refugees were paying passengers and must be treated well. He did not harbour anti-Semitic beliefs and even went so far as to remove a large formal portrait of Adolf Hitler from the ship's ballroom so the room could be used as a place for Jewish worship. It was a politically dangerous move.

Schröder kept a meticulous journal, logging the journey, his thoughts, and apprehensions. After the *St. Louis*'s first day at sea he wrote:

Gustav Schröder began his career in 1902 at age sixteen, and became a captain in 1926. He was widely respected both in life and after his death in 1959.

There is a somewhat nervous disposition among the passengers. Despite this, everyone seems convinced they will never see Germany again. Touching departure scenes have taken place. Many seem light of heart, having left their homes. Others take it heavily. But beautiful weather, pure sea air, good food, and attentive service will soon provide the usual worry-free atmosphere of long sea voyages. Painful impressions on land disappear quickly at sea and soon seem merely like dreams.

For Sol, the two-week voyage to Cuba was filled with happiness. He was six years old, and could swim in the pool and play

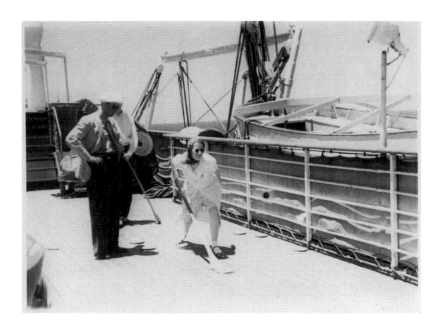

Passengers pass the time by playing shuffleboard on the main deck. COURTESY OF THE UNITED STATES HOLOCAUST MEMORIAL MUSEUM

with the other children aboard the luxury liner. For his parents, there was music, dancing, good food, and movies. Sol's family was not wealthy—their room was in third class—but that didn't matter. For the first time in a long time, Sol felt like he was being treated like a real person. "We were treated beautifully," Sol recalled. "We were on a cruise. It was fantastic."

Everything changed as they approached Havana, Cuba. One day before arriving in the city's harbour, Captain Schröder received a cable from the Hamburg-America Line's office which stated: "Majority of your passengers in contravention of new Cuban Law… may not be given permission to disembark…you will maintain speed and course, as situation is not completely clear but certainly critical if not resolved before your arrival." The owners of the *St. Louis* had known even before the ship set sail from Europe that its

Sol (centre) onboard the MS *St. Louis* with his parents in 1939. COURTESY OF THE
UNITED STATES HOLOCAUST MEMORIAL MUSEUM

passengers might have trouble disembarking in Cuba, but hadn't
told the captain. Suddenly, Schröder was faced with the terrible re-
ality that nearly all of his passengers were forbidden to enter Cuba.
When the *St. Louis* arrived in Havana on May 27, 1939, instead
of being allowed to dock and let its passengers off, the ship was
forced to simply float in the harbour and hope Cuba's government
officials would change their minds.

DISAPPOINTMENT IN CUBA

Captain Schröder learned that a new Cuban official order nullified
the landing permits most of his passengers held. In Havana, the *St.
Louis* passengers were informed that the Cuban government had
decided to cancel their entry visas. The passengers were unaware

REPUBLICA DE CUBA

DEPARTAMENTO DE INMIGRACION

TARJETA DE IDENTIFICACION DEL PASAJERO TRANSEUNTE
—IDENTIFICATION CARD OF THE PASSENGER INTRANSIT.

Nombre del pasajero .... Alma Seligmann
Name of passenger

Nacionalidad ... Alemana .... Nombre del Vapor ,, "St. Louis"
Nationality   Name of Steamer

Manifesto No. .... 4 .... Partida No. 21
Manifest No.   Line No.

Puerto de procedencia del pasajero .... Hamburg
Port of origin of the passenger.

AVISOS: 1.—Esta tarjeta deberá ser conservada por el pasajero para su identificación en Cuba.
2.—Transcurridos 90 días de la llegada del turista o transeunte, y sin perjuicio de lo que disponen las Leyes sobre Inmigración, deberá inscribirse en el "Registro de Extranjeros".
3.—El portador se obliga a no desempeñar empleo ni trabajo de ninguna clase en Cuba.

NOTICE: 1.—This card must be retained by the person to whom is issued for purposes of identification during the permanency in, and departure from Cuba.
2.—Upon arrival in Cuba the person to whom this card is issued agrees to comply with and conform to the Laws of Immigration, and 90 days after date of arrival must register at the "Registration Bureau for Aliens"
3.—The holder also agrees not to engage in pursuit of work or employment in any shape or form, paid by any person or Company established in Cuba, during his, or her, permanency in Cuba.

Fecha .... 27. Mai 1939
Date.

Firma del pasajero *Alma Seligmann* ... Sobrecargo *Otto Müller*
Passenger's signature   Purser.

ect 39 ld   P 89 a

An immigration identification card issued by the Cuban Department of Immigration to *St. Louis* passenger Alma Seligmann. COURTESY OF THE UNITED STATES HOLOCAUST MEMORIAL MUSEUM

that earlier that year, the government had issued Decree 55, which stated that every immigrant entering Cuba required a five-hundred-dollar bond to guarantee that he or she would not become a financial burden on the country. Decree 55 also stated that tourists and those only staying in Cuba for a brief time were welcome, and did not need visas or to post a bond. Benitez Gonzalez had taken advantage of this loophole. He sold "tourist landing permits" to people like the passengers onboard the *St. Louis*, who were not tourists, but refugees. He pocketed their money knowing they would never be legally allowed to enter the country.

A week before the *St. Louis* sailed, Cuban President Federico Laredo Brú issued another decree that invalidated all landing certificates issued by Benitez Gonzalez. The passengers became

So close, yet so far: the view of downtown Havana from the deck of the *St. Louis*. COURTESY OF THE UNITED STATES HOLOCAUST MEMORIAL MUSEUM

victims of the infighting within the Cuban government and rising anti-Semitism in Cuba. Reports about the ship's voyage fuelled a large anti-Semitic demonstration in Havana on May 8, five days before the *St. Louis* sailed from Hamburg. Succumbing to the propaganda of the German government and anti-Semitic demonstrations in Cuba, the Cuban government refused to allow the ship to dock when it arrived.

When the *St. Louis* arrived in Havana Harbor on May 27, the Cuban government allowed twenty-eight passengers to leave the ship: twenty-two were Jewish and had valid US visas; the remaining six—four Spanish citizens and two Cubans—had legitimate Cuban entry documents. The rest of the passengers, who were holding the worthless "Benitez Certificates," as they became known, were told they had to wait. There was nothing else they could do. Confusion and panic broke out onboard the *St. Louis*. If forced to return to Germany, the passengers knew they would likely face death.

Docked for several days in the Havana Harbor, Sol remembers the oppressive heat and the fear that quickly spread across the ship.

Boats filled with journalists and relatives of passengers filled Havana's harbour while everyone awaited the government's decision. COURTESY OF THE UNITED STATES HOLOCAUST MEMORIAL MUSEUM

"Everyone was scared to death," he said. Some passengers were so anxious that they jumped overboard in desperation and attempted to swim to shore. One passenger, Max Loewe, a veteran of the First World War, became so deeply depressed about having been denied entry into Cuba that he slashed his wrists with a straight razor and leapt over the ship's railing. A crewmember saved him from drowning and Max was taken to a hospital in Havana.

The media in the Cuban capital told the story of the attempted suicide and distributed it worldwide by telegraph. Before long, the MS *St. Louis* and its stranded Jewish refugees became an international news story. Boats filled with journalists floated in the harbour, each hoping to speak with the passengers. Sympathetic stories appeared in newspapers around the world. On June 9, 1939, an editorial in the *New York Times* called the *St. Louis* "the saddest

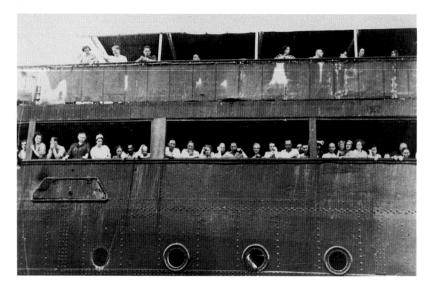

Jewish refugees aboard the *St. Louis* attempt to communicate with friends and relatives in Cuba, who were permitted to approach the vessel in small boats.
COURTESY OF THE UNITED STATES HOLOCAUST MEMORIAL MUSEUM

ship afloat today," and went on to wax poetic about the motivations behind denying the Jewish refugees safe haven: "Perhaps Cuba, as her spokesmen say, has already taken too many German refugees. Yet all these 900 asked was a temporary haven."

Some of the other boats in Havana's harbour were filled with relatives of the ship's passengers. Sol remembers his aunts, uncles, and cousins—who had left Europe months earlier and found safety in Cuba—renting a fishing boat to visit them at the ship. Separated by water and talking through the porthole in their cabin or from the ship's deck, Sol's family members caught up on each other's lives and exchanged gifts. But Sol and his parents could not leave the ship.

After days of unsuccessful governmental negotiations, Captain Schröder had no choice but to begin the return trip to Germany. There was nowhere else to go. Not wanting to return to Europe

The announcement Captain Schröder posted after his failed negotiations in Cuba. It reads: "The Cuban government is forcing us to leave the port. They have permitted us to stay here until daybreak and the departure is set for 10:00 Friday morning. The departure has not brought about any disruption in the negotiations. Only the situation brought about by the departure of the ship is a precondition for the intervention of Mr. Berenson and his co-workers. The ship administration will remain in further contact with all Jewish organizations and all other governmental offices, and will, with all available means, seek a remedy, so that a disembarkation outside Germany will occur, and we will stay for the time being near the American coast." COURTESY OF THE UNITED STATES HOLOCAUST MEMORIAL MUSEUM

immediately, Captain Schröder delayed the trip by sailing around the coast of Florida, just outside of American territory, hopeful the US authorities would allow the *St. Louis* to dock.

One night while standing on the ship's deck with his father, Sol saw lights in the distance. "What are those lights?" he remembers

asking. His father told him it was Miami, Florida. Physically, they were so close to the city but in that moment, getting there felt as impossible as flying to the moon.

TURNING BACK

Despite some public pressure and the efforts of a few members of President Franklin D. Roosevelt's cabinet, the United States wouldn't allow the *St. Louis*'s passengers to enter the country, citing existing immigration guidelines regarding entry visas.

On June 7, less than a month after departing Germany, Captain Schröder reluctantly turned the ship back to Europe. The small group of Canadians who had made valiant efforts to provide sanctuary for the passengers had been unsuccessful. Showing humanity and empathy for his Jewish passengers, Captain Schröder planned to beach the ship on the English coast rather than return to Germany where he was certain they would be killed.

Captain Schröder, who had written to Cuban president Federico Laredo Brú to say that he would not be responsible for the fate of the refugees if they returned to Germany, posted what he intended to be an encouraging message for passengers onboard the

The Meyersteins, one of the many young families on the MS *St. Louis*.
COURTESY OF THE UNITED STATES HOLOCAUST MEMORIAL MUSEUM

BESUCHERKARTE   J11
BEZOEKKAART
PERMIS DE VISITE

S/S - M/S   *Rhakotis*

Vorname & Name
des Besuchers

Am _____ von _____ bis _____

Unterschrift des Besuchers: Aussteller :

Die Besucher müssen diese Karte an Bord auf Verlangen vorzeigen und das Schiff spätestens eine Stunde vor Abfahrt verlassen haben.
De bezoekers moeten deze kaart op aanvraag toonen en het schip ten laatste één uur voor het vertrek verlaten hebben.
Les Visiteurs doivent présenter cette carte à bord sur demande et avoir quitté le navire au plus tard une heure avant l'heure du départ.

EIFFE & Cᵒ,   LANGE NIEUWSTRAAT, 43,   ANTWERPEN
MEIR, 24ᵉ

A visitor's permit issued by the HAPAG shipping company allowing passengers from the *St. Louis* to disembark at the port of Antwerp, Belgium. COURTESY OF THE UNITED STATES HOLOCAUST MEMORIAL MUSEUM

St. Louis. It read: "The shipping company is going to remain in touch with various organizations and official bodies which will endeavor to effect [*sic*] a landing outside Germany. We shall try to stay somewhere in [the] vicinity of South American countries." The message did little to comfort them. A committee of passengers was formed to prevent suicides.

Captain Schröder later described a game he saw some children playing onboard during the trip back to Europe. Two small boys with strict expressions guarded a barrier they had constructed out of chairs. Other children lined up asking to be let through.

"Are you a Jew?" asked one of the guards.

"Yes," replied a child standing by the barrier.

"Jews not admitted!" yelled the guard.

"Oh, please let me in. I'm only a very little Jew."

ARRIVING BACK IN EUROPE

On June 13, as the ship reached the halfway point on its voyage back to Europe, Morris Troper, chief of European operations for the American Jewish Joint Distribution Committee (JDC),

Mr. and Mrs. Morris Troper (centre) pose with Jewish refugees on the deck of the MS *St. Louis* after the ship arrived in the port of Antwerp. COURTESY OF
THE UNITED STATES HOLOCAUST MEMORIAL MUSEUM

a Jewish humanitarian assistance organization, brokered a solution. Troper sent a letter announcing that passengers would disembark in Belgium and from there, they would be dispersed to four western European countries willing to accommodate them.

The message Troper wired the passengers' committee aboard the *St. Louis* read: "Final arrangements for disembarkation all passengers completed. Happy [to] inform you governments of Belgium, Holland, France and England cooperated magnificently with American Joint Distribution Committee."

The passengers swiftly replied with this message: "The 907 passengers of *St. Louis* dangling for last thirteen days between hope and despair received today your liberating message…our gratitude is as immense as the ocean on which we are now floating since

St. Louis Captain Gustav Schröder negotiates landing permits for his passengers with Belgian officials. COURTESY OF THE UNITED STATES HOLOCAUST MEMORIAL MUSEUM

Passengers crowd on the deck of the *St. Louis* as the ship approaches the Port of Antwerp, Belgium, on June 17, 1939. COURTESY OF THE UNITED STATES HOLOCAUST MEMORIAL MUSEUM

THE *ST. LOUIS* IN POPULAR CULTURE

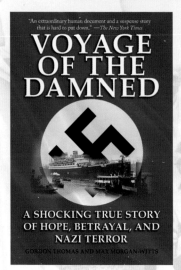

"An extraordinary human document and a suspense story that is hard to put down." —*The New York Times*

VOYAGE OF THE DAMNED

A SHOCKING TRUE STORY OF HOPE, BETRAYAL, AND NAZI TERROR

GORDON THOMAS AND MAX MORGAN-WITTS

The 1974 novel was inspired by the true events of the MS *St. Louis*. REPRODUCED BY PERMISSION OF SKYHORSE PUBLISHING, INC.

Much has been written in popular culture about the MS *St. Louis* and its tragic voyage. Gordon Thomas and Max Morgan-Witts wrote a book, *Voyage of the Damned*, in 1974. Two years later it was adapted into a Hollywood movie. Starring Faye Dunaway and Orson Welles, *Voyage of the Damned* was nominated for three Academy Awards and six Golden Globes, winning one for Best Supporting Actress in a Motion Picture (Katharine Ross).

In 2009, American cartoonist Art Spiegelman, author of the Pulitzer Prize-winning graphic novel *Maus*, drew a full-page comic strip about the MS *St. Louis* for the *Washington Post*. The thought-provoking panels were published to commemorate the seventieth anniversary of the ship's voyage.

In 2010, Sarah A. Ogilvie and Scott Miller of the United States Holocaust Memorial Museum set out to discover what happened to each of the 937 passengers onboard the *St. Louis*. Their investigation, which spanned ten years and took them halfway around the world, resulted in a book called *Refuge Denied: The St. Louis Passengers and the Holocaust*.

May 13 first full of hope for a good future and afterwards in the deepest despair. Accept…the deepest and eternal thanks of men women and children united by the same fate on board the *St. Louis*."

France agreed to take in 224 refugees; Belgium, 214; the Netherlands, 181; and England, 287. (Max Loewe, who was still recovering in a Havana hospital, was eventually shipped to England, bringing the total *St. Louis* passengers in Britain to 288.)

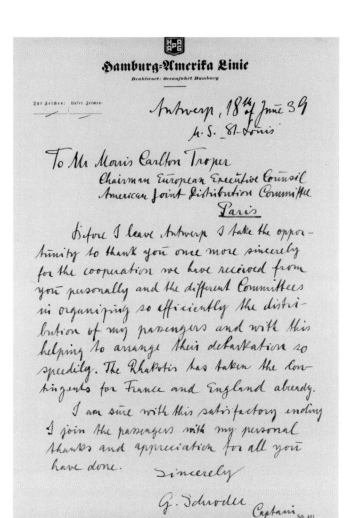

The handwritten letter Captain Schröder sent to Morris Troper. It reads: "Before I leave Antwerp I take the opportunity to thank you once more sincerely for the cooperation we have received from you personally and the different Committees in organizing so efficiently the distribution of my passengers and with this helping to arrange their debarkation so speedily. The *Rhuputis* has taken the contingents for France and England already. I am sure with this satisfactory ending I join the passengers with my personal thanks and appreciation for all you have done."

Jubilant passengers disembark in Antwerp after more than a month at sea.
COURTESY OF THE UNITED STATES HOLOCAUST MEMORIAL MUSEUM

Gustav Schröder received many honours after the war. He died in 1959, but in 1993, the State of Israel gave him the title of "Righteous Among the Nations." In 2000, a city street in Hamburg was named after him and a detailed plaque unveiled.

On June 17, 1939, the *St. Louis* docked at Antwerp, Belgium. Initially relieved, the passengers soon realized that as the Second World War raged on, they were anything but safe back in Europe.

Sol and his family were allowed to disembark in Antwerp. While in Belgium, Jewish humanitarian organizations helped the family by providing food and shelter, and assisting with paperwork as they waited for their United States visa numbers to come up. But the Germans were moving toward Brussels, and the Messingers they knew they couldn't stay. Sol's father threw a few of their personal belongings into a bedsheet and the family left in May 1940. They boarded a train to Paris and eventually made their way in a cattle car to a small village called Savignac in the Pyrenees Mountains in southern France on the border with Spain.

AGDE INTERNMENT CAMP

The Messinger family had been in Savignac three months when French police rounded up all the Jewish refugees in the area and took them to Agde, a French internment camp near Montpellier in southern France. "It wasn't an extermination camp," Sol recalled, but life at the camp was difficult. Sol remembers sleeping on hay in a barracks and eating soup that wasn't much more than water. Men and women were segregated and children stayed with their mothers. Once a week, Sol saw his father through a barbed-wire fence.

Helped by Jews outside the camp, Sol and his mother, along with a few others, managed to escape. It was Christmas Eve and the guards were drinking and having a party. Sol's father escaped the camp not long afterwards, on New Year's Eve. The family was reunited and spent the next year and half in Savignac. Sol's father worked as a tailor, and the family saved money and waited.

HEADING TO AMERICA

In the spring of 1942, the Messingers' American visa number finally came up. They left Europe from Portugal aboard the *Serpa Pinto*, a small cargo ship. Unlike his voyage on the grand *St. Louis*, this trip was not pleasurable for Sol. He felt every ocean swell on the *Serpa Pinto* and spent the entire trip to the United States seasick. Since they were under the constant threat of German submarine attacks, the trip took longer than normal.

Sol and his family finally arrived in New York City on June 24, 1942. Several relatives who had come to the United States through Cuba years earlier welcomed them. Two of Sol's aunts had settled in Buffalo, New York, and his family made their way to that city. Before long, Sol started school. He learned English and played sports; his life began to resemble that of a typical American child.

The still-hopeful Heilbrun family aboard the MS *St. Louis* **before they were denied entry to Cuba.** COURTESY OF THE UNITED STATES HOLOCAUST MEMORIAL MUSEUM

Sol eventually became a doctor and raised his own family, but he never forgot his life in Europe under the Nazis or how close he came to death when his family was turned back from Cuba in 1939. He knew that he could have easily been among the more than 250 refugees aboard the *St. Louis* who later died in the Holocaust.

Of the *St. Louis* passengers who returned to continental Europe, researchers for the United States Holocaust Memorial Museum have determined that 87 emigrated before Germany invaded Western Europe on May 10, 1940. After that date, 254 passengers who had disembarked the *St. Louis* in Belgium, France, and the Netherlands died during the Holocaust. Most of them were murdered in the extermination camps at Auschwitz and Sobibór, and the rest died in concentration or internment camps, in hiding, or attempting to evade the Nazis.

Around half of the original 937 refugees onboard the *St. Louis* are known to have eventually migrated to the United States. Some made their way to Canada, Argentina, Australia, Brazil, Mexico, and other countries.

"It is one of the most shameful periods in American history," said Sol. But he holds no bitterness toward the country that eventually welcomed his family and became his home. "Like every person, like every country, they make mistakes."

An illustration of the Hamburg-America Line's pier in Hoboken, New Jersey:
a regular port of call. COURTESY OF HERITAGE SHIPS

CHAPTER 3

CANADIANS PETITION THE GOVERNMENT

AFTER CUBA AND THE UNITED STATES denied safe haven to the hundreds of Jewish refugees onboard the MS *St. Louis*, Halifax remained the last possible port of asylum in North America for the frightened passengers. Canada became one of their last hopes for rescue from Nazi persecution in Europe.

The city of Halifax was founded in 1749, during a period known as the Golden Age of Sail. Ships carrying goods and people from around the world arrived in Halifax Harbour and helped establish strong trading links with Britain, the United States, and the West Indies. The Golden Age of Sail lasted from the sixteenth to the mid-nineteenth century and was a time when international trade and naval warfare were dominated by ships.

With the outbreak of the First World War in 1914, the role of the port took on new importance. The Halifax port more than proved its worth by ferrying goods, supplies, and soldiers to the front in Europe. In 1918, the *London Times* called Halifax "the third most important port in the World."

With all the dangerous munitions and explosive cargo travelling in and out of the port of Halifax, the potential for catastrophe was never far away. In 1917, the *Mont–Blanc*, a French munitions ship was leaving the Bedford Basin to join a convoy across the Atlantic when it was struck by the *Imo*, a vessel carrying relief supplies destined for Belgium. The resulting explosion, known now as the Halifax Explosion, was massive—it killed two thousand people, flattened the city's north end, and destroyed much of the port infrastructure.

In the aftermath of the explosion, port expansion plans that had been drawn up before the war were revisited. Government officials agreed to develop an enormous terminal in the city's south end, adjacent to the harbour's entrance. Between 1921 and 1928, new facilities called the Ocean Terminals, along with a grain elevator and cold storage facility, were built.

Halifax's Ocean Terminals later expanded to include Piers 26 and 28, as well as Pier B. The deep water meant the terminals could handle the largest vessels in the world. Three ships could dock at once, and the facilities boasted what port officials called "the finest passenger traffic accommodation on the Western Atlantic coast."

Although a few immigrants began arriving at Pier 21 in 1924, it did not officially open until March 8, 1928, when the *Nieuw Amsterdam* docked, becoming the first immigrant ship to arrive at the newly opened facility.

PETITIONS

A petition is a formal written request, typically one signed by many people, appealing to an authority (such as a government) about a particular issue or cause.

One of the most famous petitions in Canadian history involved five women from Alberta who became known as the Famous Five or the Valiant Five. In 1927, the five women—Emily Murphy, Irene Parlby, Nellie McClung, Louise McKinney, and Henrietta Edwards—created a petition asking the Supreme Court of Canada to answer the question, "Does the word 'persons' in Section 24 of the British North America Act of 1867, include female 'persons?'" They wanted women to be legally recognized as persons that they could be appointed to the senate, which at that time only allowed men. In 1928, Canada's Supreme Court responded to the petition by delivering its unanimous decision that women were not such "persons." It would be two more years before Canada had its first female senator.

According to *The Pier 21 Story*, a short history pulled together by Public Affairs Nova Scotia, the situation was finally rectified in 1924: "Facilities were opened adjoining the temporary south end railway station in a large airy building that for more than forty years would bear the name, familiar to hundreds of thousands of immigrants, of Pier 21."

While the ship was sailing within two days of Halifax in early June 1939, leaders of Canada's Jewish community and a small group of non-Jews pleaded with the federal government to provide sanctuary to the Jewish passengers. They had been following the ship's plight in the news. One article in the *New York Times* read: "We can only hope that some hearts will soften somewhere and some refuge be found. The cruise of the *St. Louis* [cries] to heaven of man's inhumanity to man."

On June 7, 1939, a group led by George Wrong, an influential ordained priest and historian at the University of Toronto, sent a telegram to Prime Minister Mackenzie King begging that he show "true Christian charity" and offer the Jewish passengers a safe home in Canada. The petition was sent the same day Captain Schröder reluctantly pointed the *St. Louis* back in the direction of Europe.

Toronto, Ont., June 7, 1939
Right Hon. W. L. Mackenzie King, P.C.

As a mark of gratitude to almighty God for the pleasure and gratification which has been vouchsafed the Canadian people through the visit [of] their Gracious Majesties King George and Queen Elizabeth and as evidence of the true Christian charity of the people of this most fortunate and blessed country we the undersigned as Christian citizens of Canada respectfully suggest that under the powers vested in you as Premier of our country you forwith [*sic*] offer to the 907 homeless exiles on board the Hamburg-American ship *St. Louis* sanctuary in Canada.

George M. Wrong
Elizabeth Wrong
[etc.]

The June 7 petition was signed by thirty-seven influential women and men in Toronto, including lawyers, doctors, academics, and clergymen. B. K. Sandwell of *Saturday Night* magazine; Robert Falconer, past president of the University of Toronto; and Ellsworth Flavelle, a wealthy businessman, all signed. George Wrong, the petition's organizer, had strong connections to the country's Liberal party: he was married to Elizabeth Blake, daughter of Edward Blake, a prominent member of Canada's first Liberal government from 1873 to 1882. George and Elizabeth's son, Humphrey Wrong, was a prominent diplomat who had served as Canada's representative at the 1938 Evian Conference on the question of Jewish refugees: where they would go, and how best to help them. Delegates from thirty-two countries and relief organizations met in Évian-les-Bains, France, to come up with a long-term solution to the problem.

But Wrong's connections, credentials, and the influential signatures on his petition weren't enough to change the prime minister's mind. King's government was firmly opposed to admitting the passengers of the *St. Louis* solely on humanitarian grounds and claimed the refugees did not qualify as admissible immigrants under Canada's immigration law.

CANADA'S RESPONSE TO THE PETITION

Before responding to Wrong's petition, Oscar Skelton, Canada's undersecretary of state for foreign affairs, wrote to the prime minister. In a confidential correspondence with King dated June 9, 1939, Skelton notes that the *St. Louis* had reportedly already set sail on its return voyage to Europe. Skelton noted in his correspondence that since January 1939, of the twelve hundred immigrants admitted to Canada under special Orders-in-Council (because they did not fit regular immigration criteria), "Jews comprised sixty per cent." But, he added, "No publicity has been given it."

Ten days later, Skelton responded to Wrong's petition by letter, stating that Canada had not received any formal requests to land from the *St. Louis*. Skelton offered a summary of Canada's immigration policy, saying it focused on permanent, agricultural immigrants and people with "investment capital" or technical and scientific expertise. He used the policy as justification for the government's decision to refuse Wrong's demand that the refugees be admitted to Canada.

Ottawa, June 19th, 1939
Dear Dr. Wrong,

I wish to refer to your telegram of June 7th to the Prime Minister and the further exchange of telegrams on June 8th regarding the proposal that the Canadian government should admit to Canada the 907 refugees on board the Hamburg-American Line's *St. Louis*.

The proposal was given immediate consideration. While every sympathy was felt with the unfortunate position in which the refugees in question found themselves, it was regretted it was not possible to recommend their admission en bloc into Canada.

The refugees on board the *St. Louis* were in practically all cases seeking admission into the United States…They had secured or thought they had secured permission to land in Cuba and remain there temporarily while qualifying for admission to the United States. The Cuban authorities declined to admit them on the ground that their permits had been issued irregularly in Europe; notification of their cancellation was stated by the Cuban authorities to have been notified to the steamship authorities before the vessel sailed. In addition to the *St. Louis* other vessels sailing from German ports have recently carried considerable numbers of passengers to America or Asiatic ports who on arrival were found ineligible for immediate entry.

None of the passengers on the *St. Louis*, so far as our authorities were aware, had previously indicated a desire to enter Canada and no request for permission to land here was received from the ship or passengers or from the Joint Distribution Committee in charge of their movements. The immediate difficulties in which they found themselves were due to the working of the United States quota system in conjunction with the revision of the Cuban system of temporary admission.

The Canadian government has not adopted the quota system of admission as the United States has done. It does not admit immigrants for temporary purposes in order to qualify themselves for entrance to other countries as has until recently been the practice in Cuba. Neither does it admit immigrants temporarily as was done in a number of the Western European countries subject to the provision that they must not seek employment....

Yours Sincerely,
O. D. Skelton

FREDERICK BLAIR'S
ANTI-SEMITIC SENTIMENTS

Months before organizing the June petition, George Wrong had written to the prime minister about the desperate situation facing German Jewish refugees. In that letter, he noted that Canada had "vast empty territory," but that its population suffered from "a sense of remoteness from the urgency of the problem." In a letter of reply, Prime Minister Mackenzie King had promised Canada would contribute in some way to solving "the most baffling of our international problems." His response was vague, but he expressed some apprehension, saying that it would be necessary to determine "how far it is possible to go, without raising a condition which it may be more difficult to meet than the one it is intended to cure."

Jewish refugees were far from the prime minister's mind when Wrong sent the petition in June. King was in Washington, accompanying King George VI and Queen Elizabeth (later the Queen Mother) on the final leg of their grand North American tour. The tour was historic for Canada: it was the first time a reigning monarch had visited the country. In the prime minister's mind, the *St. Louis* was not a Canadian problem. But when finally confronted

with it, he said he would consult with Frederick Blair, the director of Canada's immigration branch.

Known for his anti-Semitic sentiments, Blair said that the Jewish refugees did not qualify under immigration laws. Canada had already done too much for the Jews, he added. No country could "open its doors wide enough to take in the hundreds of thousands of Jewish people who want to leave Europe: the line must be drawn somewhere," he said.

CANADA'S CLOSED DOORS

Prime Minister King knew that Canadians didn't want boatloads of Jewish refugees landing in Halifax, and Canada had its own domestic problems in the late 1930s. The country was in an economic crisis, part of the worldwide economic down-turn that became known as the Great Depression. The timing of the Great Depression varied across nations, but in most countries it started in 1929 and lasted until the late 1930s. It was the longest, deepest, and most widespread of the twentieth century.

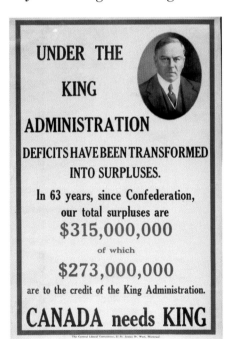

A Mackenzie King election poster, 1930.

The economic crisis slowed down almost all immigration to Canada, and there was rampant anti-Semitism across the country. Canada's door was

A French-language election poster showing Prime Minister King using a hammer of "conciliation" to create "goodwill," 1930. LIBRARY AND ARCHIVES CANADA

essentially closed by 1933 and opened only slightly by 1948. For Jews, it was only opened a crack. After 1948, when the European Jewish refugee crisis lessened with the creation of the state of Israel, Canada began lifting its barriers against Jewish immigration.

King understood that allowing Jewish refugees into Canada was unpopular and threatened his chance for re-election. He was particularly concerned about Quebec and its French-speaking voters. In Quebec, anti-Jewish sentiment was strong in the 1930s. Catholic priests in Quebec preached anti-Semitic messages about Jews murdering Jesus Christ, and many Quebecers living in poor rural areas believed the Nazi lies about Jews controlling international finances. Finally, Quebecers feared the province's distinct culture would be undermined because Jewish immigrants would want to learn English instead of French.

Even the outbreak of the Second World War and the mounting evidence of the Nazis' plan for the total annihilation of European Jews did not move Canada to open its doors. There was no groundswell of opposition and no humanitarian appeal for a more open policy. Few Canadians saw Jews as desirable immigrants. Jews, many believed, would not "fit" into the country.

Still, some Canadian newspapers were critical of the government's "cowardly" policy toward Jewish refugees, and editorials on the subject appeared throughout the spring and summer of 1939. "Canada is missing the boat on the refugee question," wrote the *Winnipeg Free Press* on July 19, 1939. The *Globe and Mail* stated: "Canada too needs the industries that refugees are bringing to the United States. There is a need for the talents and crafts that our xenophobia has so far restricted."

THE AMERICAN RESPONSE

While leaders of Canada's Jewish community and some non-Jews pleaded with the government to provide sanctuary to the Jewish

American president Franklin Delano Roosevelt at his desk in the White House in 1935, preparing to address his nation over the radio. LIBRARY OF CONGRESS PUBLIC ARCHIVES (PHOTO BY HARRIS & EWING)

passengers onboard the *St. Louis*, impassioned American citizens also wrote letters to US president Franklin D. Roosevelt. Dee Nye, an eleven-year-old girl from Tacoma, Washington, wrote a heart-breaking letter to First Lady Eleanor Roosevelt:

> Mother of Our Country,
> I am so sad the Jewish people have to suffer so. Please let them land in America...It hurts me so that I would give them my little bed if it was the last thing I had...We have three rooms we do not use. My mother would be glad to let someone have them.

President Roosevelt received many urgent telegrams from passengers onboard the *St. Louis* pleading for refuge, but he never responded. The State Department and the White House had decided not to take extraordinary measures to permit the refugees to enter the United States. On June 4, 1939, A. M. Warren of the State Department's Visa Division formally shut out the *St. Louis* passengers. "The German refugees," he said in a statement, "must await their turn [for their formal waiting numbers to come up] before they may be admissible to the United States."

The United States had already reached the number of immigrants from Germany it would accept that year. This quota, established by the 1924 Immigration Act, firmly limited the number of immigrants by nationality that would be admitted to the United States during any given year. The quota for German refugees in 1939 was 27,370.

President Roosevelt also had the opportunity to accept a proposal allowing Jewish refugees a temporary safe haven in the US Virgin Islands. In 1938, the islands' governor and legislative assembly even extended an offer to accept them, according to Rafael Medoff, director of the Washington-based David S. Wyman Institute for Holocaust Studies. US Secretary of the Treasury Henry Morgenthau, Junior proposed the *St. Louis* passengers be allowed to stay in the Virgin Islands temporarily on tourist visas, but President Roosevelt disagreed, claiming Nazi spies disguised as refugees might try to infiltrate the the United States.

President Roosevelt could have also issued an executive order to admit the passengers of the *St. Louis* on an emergency basis, but that would have posed several problems. First, it would have been unfair to the approximately twenty-five hundred Jews who were already waiting in Cuba, as well as the thousands in Europe who had applied for American visas. It would have also triggered a huge negative reaction toward Roosevelt's government from the country's powerful anti-immigrant lobby group. And it probably would have encouraged more ships to circumvent the country's immigration policy to gain direct admission to the United States.

While some criticized President Roosevelt for failing to take decisive action, others argued that his lack of action was understandable given the circumstances.

CANADA'S POOR RECORD

Canada was clearly not alone in its failure to take decisive action when confronted with the opportunity to help Jewish refugees. The country's anti-Jewish immigration policy, imposed by Prime Minister Mackenzie King and Immigration Director Frederick Blair, gave Canada one of the worst records among western countries in helping those suffering under Nazism. By comparison, Bolivia, a Central American country smaller than Canada in both population and geographical size, would admit around thirty thousand Jewish immigrants between 1938 and 1941. About eighty-five thousand Jewish refugees reached the United States between March 1938 and September 1939, still far below the number of people seeking refuge. Canada allowed in only five thousand Jewish immigrants between 1933 and 1948. Historian Irving Abella described it as a "hideous, shameful, disgraceful record."

An anti-Nazi button manufactured in North America, c. 1942. COURTESY OF THE UNITED STATES HOLOCAUST MEMORIAL MUSEUM

When Canadians became aware, through the press, of the mass deportations, concentration camps, and the full extent of the horrors Jews faced in the Holocaust, they—for the most part—were embarrassed by their government's decision to deny a safe haven to the hundreds of Jewish refugees aboard the *St. Louis*. While the anti-Jewish actions of the Nazis were reported before the war, the outbreak of fighting made getting information more difficult. It took a little less than a year after the murder of Jews started for the details of mass killings to start reaching west. The first reports about the Nazi plan for the mass murder of Jews were smuggled out of Poland by *Bund*, a Jewish socialist political organization, and reached England in the spring of 1942.

Canada's first female senator, the Honourable Cairine Wilson, sat for this oil portrait in 1930. LIBRARY AND ARCHIVES CANADA

CHAPTER 4

CAIRINE WILSON'S VALIANT BATTLE

"We must be big enough and courageous enough to admit to Canada a fair share of the unfortunate persons involved."

—CAIRINE WILSON

IN THE LATE 1930S THERE was a small group of Canadians who refused to remain quiet about the growing atrocities Jewish citizens were facing in Europe. Across the country, they protested against Hitler and his anti-Semitic laws by holding public demonstrations, hoping to push the Canadian government to take action and help the growing number of Jewish refugees in Europe.

One of the leading voices in Canada was Cairine Wilson. A persistent and determined Christian woman, Wilson was a peace activist, humanitarian, mother of eight, and one of the few non-Jews lobbying on behalf of the refugees. For her work, she earned the title "Mother of the Refugees."

Appointed to Canada's senate in 1930 at age forty-five, Wilson was the country's first female senator. In the late 1930s, she was probably the most active parliamentarian on the issue of Jewish refugees.

Frederick Blair, the country's top immigration official at the time, had a lot of power in determining who got into Canada. After Prime Minister Mackenzie King's Liberals came to power in 1935, Blair, as director of the Immigration Branch of the Department of Mines and Resources, was tasked with ensuring that restrictions on immigration were upheld. A religious man, an elder in his church, and a dedicated civil servant, Blair mirrored the increasingly anti-immigration spirit of the times.

REFUGEE: ANOTHER WORD FOR JEW

For Blair, the term "refugee" was really just another word for "Jew." Unless safeguards were adopted, he warned, Canada was in danger of being "flooded by Jewish people." He saw his task as ensuring the safeguards didn't fail.

Blair wasn't afraid to publicly express his strong dislike for Jews but he didn't consider himself an anti-Semite; he believed he was simply being realistic about Canada's immigration needs. "I often think that instead of persecution it would be far better if we more often told them frankly why many of them are unpopular," Blair said, referring to Jews. "If they would divest themselves of certain of their habits I am sure they could be just as popular in Canada as our Scandinavians."

Blair's deeply held beliefs weren't that different from many other Canadians at the time. Anti-Semitism ran strong throughout Canadian society. In the 1930s, the Jewish community in Canada was small, making up less than 1.5 percent of Canada's total population of 11 million. Despite their small numbers, Jews often shouldered the blame for many of the country's economic problems. They were subjected to strict quotas in employment, education, and housing. Many businesses wouldn't hire Jews, and Jewish professionals were often excluded from jobs at universities, hospitals, and law firms. Clubs, resorts, and beaches also barred Jewish Canadians.

According to American Gallup surveys conducted between 1938 and 1939, three-fifths of respondents found Jews to have "objectionable characteristics." Between 12 and 15 percent of those responding were prepared to support anti-Semitic campaigns.

Former prime minister Richard Bedford Bennett (L) and Prime Minister William Lyon Mackenzie King, c. 1933. LIBRARY AND ARCHIVES CANADA

North of the border, fiercely patriotic associations such as the Canadian Corps and the Native Sons of Canada believed excluding immigrants from countries other than Great Britain was the only way to maintain the British character of the country.

CANADA'S ETHNICALLY SELECTIVE IMMIGRATION POLICIES

While immigration had been seen as essential to growing Canada's prosperity at the turn of the twentieth century, the country's policies had always been ethnically selective. The government preferred British and American immigrants and left Jews, Asians, and Blacks at the bottom of the list. Close to 3 million immigrants came to Canada during the first fifteen years of the century. The numbers peaked in 1913 with 382,841 new arrivals that year. By opening its doors to fill the vast space and provide workers to grow the country economically, in the decade between 1901 and 1911, the Canadian population jumped by 43 percent.

By the 1930s, with the country in an economic depression and more than 32 percent of Canadian workers unemployed, few questioned the government's increasingly restrictive immigration policies. The government of Prime Minister Richard Bedford (R. B.) Bennett implemented the tightest immigration admissions policy in Canadian history. The restrictions were deemed necessary to combat soaring unemployment and prevent further economic decline.

Access to Canada for most potential immigrants ended with the passage of Order-in-Council PC 695 in March 1931. It restricted admission to American citizens and British subjects who had enough money to support themselves while finding a job in Canada, agriculturalists who had the financial means to farm, and the wives and children of Canadian residents.

KEEPING THE REST OF THE WORLD OUT

According to the 1982 book *None is Too Many* by historians Irving Abella and Harold Troper, "Canada effectively closed its doors to the rest of the world. Throughout the economic turmoil of the Great Depression and the racial oppression of the Second World War, Canada remained committed to this policy of exclusion, denying entrance to both immigrants and refugees."

Fewer immigrants were arriving in Canada each year. The numbers dropped to fewer than twenty-six thousand people in 1932, down from eighty-eight thousand in 1931, according to annual reports from the Department of Mines and Resources,

Immigration Branch. In 1936, only eleven thousand people entered the country, a drop of more than 93 percent from the 1930 level. The numbers started to rise gradually in 1939 to more than seventeen thousand, but with tens of thousands of German refugees seeking safety in countries like Canada, that number was insignificant.

As anti-Semitism grew in Germany, Canada began to actively restrict Jewish-specific immigration. In 1938, the capital requirement for Jewish applicants was raised from $5,000 to $15,000 per family. But by the end of 1938, the Canadian immigration branch was even rejecting Jewish families able to bring $20,000 or more with them to Canada. As well, immigrants had to prove they were farmers, which Blair hoped would further sift out the Jewish applicants; he knew most were coming from European cities. Jewish agriculturalists who met the capital requirement were routinely rejected because, according to Blair and his officials, "experience had shown that the Jewish people do not…take to farming."

As early as 1937, the country's immigration branch was aware of the influx of refugees and its effect on traditional immigration patterns. The annual report for that year stated: "There is at present a great pressure at our doors for the admission of many thousands of distressed peoples of Europe. This pressure is greater than that created by Canada during the early years of this century when thousands of dollars were expended annually in propaganda to attract immigrants."

THE EVIAN CONFERENCE

In the United States, President Roosevelt called for global action to confront the German-Jewish refugee problem. A conference was organized and held in Évian-les-Bains, France, in July 1938. Frederick Blair told Prime Minister Mackenzie King that Canada didn't need to attend. He asserted that since 1930, the percentage

Senator Dandurand (L) and Prime Minister King at the League of Nations conference on September 29, 1936, in Geneva, Switzerland. LIBRARY AND ARCHIVES CANADA

of German Jews entering Canada exceeded the American figure by three times per capita. The director had previously said, "Efforts have been made by groups and individuals to get refugees into Canada, but we have fought all along to protect ourselves against the admission of such stateless persons without passports for the reason that coming out of the maelstrom of war, some of them are liable to go on the rocks and when they become public charges, we have to keep them for the balance of their lives."

Blair was overruled, and King sent a small Canadian delegation to the conference. The United States encouraged all countries to find a long-term solution to the problem despite the fact that the United States and most other countries were unwilling to ease their immigration restrictions. Canada, like most other countries at

the conference, feared an increase of refugees would cause further social and economic hardships. When the week-long conference ended, the Dominican Republic was the only country willing to accept more refugees.

In the end, attending the Evian Conference did little to change Canada's official stance on Jewish refugees. The prime minister feared admitting Jewish refugees might create a large social disturbance in Canada. "We must…seek," King wrote in his diary, "to keep this part of the Continent free from unrest and from too great an intermixture of foreign strains of blood." Nothing was to be gained, he believed, "by creating an internal problem in an effort to meet an international one." Allowing Jewish refugees into Canada, he told his cabinet, might cause riots and would likely exacerbate tensions between the federal government and the provinces.

King was thinking particularly about Quebec. He knew unity with French Canada was at risk since the province was reluctant to support a less restrictive immigration policy. Allowing large numbers of Jews to settle in Canada would threaten the country's unity, the prime minister believed. Canada could not simply act on humanitarian grounds—there had to be political motivation, too.

International refugee organizations grew increasingly overwhelmed. They could no longer cope with the growing problem. The League of Nations, an international peace organization, created the Commission for German Refugees, but was unable to accomplish very much. Most of the members of the league chose to either ignore or diminish the plight of the refugees. No countries came forward to accept either those refugees left in Germany or those living temporarily in surrounding European countries. "The world," said Chaim Weizmann, who later became the first president of the State of Israel, "seemed to be divided into two parts—those places where the Jew could not live, and those where they could not enter." Canada was in the latter group.

THE LEAGUE OF NATIONS

The League of Nations was an international organization established in 1919 after the First World War. Canada was a founding member. The League's main purpose was to keep peace worldwide by mediating international disputes. Even though it ultimately failed, the League laid the groundwork for future international organizational activity. It was replaced by the United Nations at the end of the Second World War.

The League of Nations Society was founded in 1921 in Canada, and promoted international peace through public education and support for the League of Nations. Headquartered in Ottawa, it operated until 1942. The society distributed League publications and sponsored speaking tours and radio broadcasts. It was the first Canadian organization to advocate for greater public awareness and understanding of international affairs.

Canada's delegation to the 1928 League of Nations meeting in Geneva, Switzerland. L–R: O. D. Skelton, Philippe Roy, Raoul Dandurand, the Right Honourable William Lyon Mackenzie King, Charles Dunning, and W. A. Riddell. LIBRARY AND ARCHIVES CANADA

CANADIANS VOCAL ABOUT REFUGEES

Canadians were passionate about both sides of the refugee issue and many wrote to their members of parliament. A number of the letters emphasized the need to stop refugees from entering the country. "It seems absurd to talk about bringing in immigrants to this country when thousands of our own people are unemployed," one Canadian wrote in 1939.

Several members of parliament echoed this sentiment. In the House of Commons in 1939, Thomas Reid, MP for New Westminster, British Columbia, argued: "[W]e should not give any encouragement to people outside our own country to come and settle on land in British Columbia. Charity begins at home, and if we have money at all to spend I think every encouragement should be given first to those in our cities who would gladly settle on the land if they were given $1,500 each."

But not all Canadians agreed. Sporadic newspaper editorials during the spring and summer of 1939 encouraged welcoming

CO-OPERATIVE COMMONWEALTH FEDERATION

The Co-operative Commonwealth Federation (CCF) was founded in Calgary in 1932. It was a political coalition of progressive, social- ist, and labour groups seeking economic reform to help Canadians deeply affected by the Great Depression. The CCF's founders were a mixture of farm organizations—such as the United Farmers of Alberta—academics, and members of parliament in Ottawa who supported farmers and trade-union organizations.

The party governed Saskatchewan under Tommy Douglas, who went on to become the first leader of the federal New Democratic Party. The CCF was eventually folded into the NDP in 1961.

While the CCF never held power nationally, it had a strong influence on Canadian politics. Many of the party's goals, such as universal health care and unemployment insurance, were adopted by the country's ruling parties and contributed to the development of Canada's welfare state.

Richard and Betty Blum, one of the many young couples on the MS *St. Louis* **who hoped to find safety in North America.** COURTESY OF THE UNITED STATES HOLOCAUST MEMORIAL MUSEUM

refugees, and pressure to liberalize the government's policy toward refugees came from a small group made up primarily of Senator Wilson, Jewish members of parliament, and the Co-operative Commonwealth Federation (CCF) Party—Canada's first social-ist party, founded in 1932.

A Jewish immigrant himself, Abraham Albert Heaps, MP for Winnipeg North during the 1930s, wrote a critical letter to Prime Minister King. "Immigration regulations in Canada are among the most stringent in the world," he wrote. "They are inhuman and unchristian…. We think it is not in keeping with good liberal doctrine to refuse the right of asylum to a limited number of political and religious refugees."

SENATOR WILSON GOES TO BATTLE

"Without a belief in the dignity of man, without indignation against arbitrarily created human suffering, there can be no democratic principles."

—Senator Cairine Wilson, in an article for *The Key*: newsletter of the Toronto Junior League, a women's organization promoting volunteerism and helping those in need

Working with various organizations, Senator Cairine Wilson began her uphill battle in the late 1930s to bring more Jewish refugees to Canada, motivated by her strong faith in humanity.

Wilson was president of the League of Nations Society in Canada, a national branch of the international organization, when she helped found the Canadian National Committee on Refugees and Victims of Persecution (CNCR) in October 1938. The CNCR was established to coordinate all efforts in Canada on behalf of refugees, and Wilson would serve as its head for the next decade.

Senator Wilson and the CNCR, with the support of organizations like the Canadian Jewish Congress and the Jewish Relief Committee (which offered to care for the European refugees if they should be admitted into the country), pleaded with Prime Minister King. Under Senator Wilson's leadership, the CNCR organized local chapters across the country, lobbied for change, and set out to educate Canadians about the plight of refugees.

A newspaper article showing German immigrant Meta Echt at the Immigrant Processing Centre at Pier 21, c. 1948. Volunteers from the Jewish Immigrant Aid Society are on hand to assist. COURTESY OF THE CANADIAN JEWISH COUNCIL

The CNCR hoped that Canadians would develop "a more sympathetic attitude toward the reception of refugees," and distributed more than nine thousand pamphlets entitled "Should Canada Admit Refugees?" Inside they stated: "it would seem fairly certain that the tragic plight of the refugees from Germany and what were formerly Austria and Czechoslovakia, could be solved if there were a genuine desire on the part of governments to do so."

Senator Wilson even banged on the doors of officials in the immigration branch to lobby for prospective refugee applicants. Each person applying for entry to Canada had to receive the individual attention of authorities. If the applicant could not fulfill all of the prerequisites, the case was rejected. Out of desperation, applicants were known to stretch the truth about their family's agricultural experience so they could qualify for admission.

"We are making some efforts in the refugee matters," Senator Wilson wrote in a letter to a friend. "I think eventually Canada may make a real contribution but it has been unexpectedly difficult to arouse public sympathy into meaningful action."

HELP FOR JEWISH ORPHANS

Knowing that Jewish children in Europe were suffering, Wilson put her greatest energy toward finding a way to help them. Certain that other Canadian mothers would feel the same, she campaigned vigorously for them to show their humanity by opening their homes to the thousands of children orphaned or separated from their families.

By the spring of 1939, more than nine thousand refugee children, many of them Jewish orphans, mainly from Germany, Austria, Poland, Czechoslovakia, and Spain, had made their way to Britain. Senator Wilson and the CNCR lobbied the Canadian government to have some of them admitted to Canada for adoption or guaranteed hospitality under the auspices of the CNCR. Faced with so much opposition, Senator Wilson was dubbed the "Mother of Lost Causes." Still, she persisted and eventually arranged for one hundred Jewish orphans residing temporarily in Britain to be accepted into Canada. Unfortunately, due to extremely strict regulations imposed by the Canadian government, only two children were ever admitted under the plan.

Wilson had more success with British children. During the summer of 1940, thanks to her work and that of many others, about fifteen hundred children from Britain, who sought refuge in Canada from the bombing in Britain, were brought to Canada under government sponsorship. After the war, Wilson continued to support government-assisted schemes to help bring children who were in danger to Canada.

The Canadian Jewish Congress also lobbied the Canadian government to allow a group of endangered Jewish orphans in France to come to Canada toward the beginning of the war. Permission was denied. Two years after the war ended, the country's immigration policies changed and orphaned Jewish children were finally allowed into Canada. An Order-in-Council passed in 1947 allowed the Canadian Jewish Congress to arrange for the

Marianne Echt (R) and her sister at their home in Poland, c. 1932: seven years before they immigrated with their family to Halifax. COURTESY OF THE CANADIAN MUSEUM OF IMMIGRATION AT PIER 21

immigration of more than one thousand orphaned Jewish children from Europe. Known as the "War Orphans Project," it continued until March 1952.

Senator Wilson's work to help refugee children did not go unnoticed. In 1950, France made her a Knight of the Legion of Honour for her courageous work on behalf of Jewish refugee children. She later became Canada's first woman delegate to the United Nations Fourth General Assembly in 1949, and worked on the committee devoted to the status of women and the United Nations International Children's Emergency Fund (UNICEF).

"You have always been a person of such great integrity," wrote Margaret Wherry, Wilson's friend and colleague. "To so many refugees you have become a friend…. To us who worked with you on various committees you were always a great source of sound and considered judgement…. Thanks for the trail you have blazed for Canadian women."

At the time of Wilson's death in March 1962, Saul Hayes, vice-president of the Canadian Jewish Congress, wrote to Senator Wilson's family expressing gratitude for her work. "The Canadian Jewish Community has cause to mourn the death of your esteemed mother whose actions on fundamental freedoms and… rights has illuminated the pages of recent Canadian history. Her life work should be the best tribute to the memory of a grand and great woman."

Marianne Echt (right) and her sister at their home in Danzig, Poland, before the Nazis came to town and began taking prisoners. COURTESY OF THE CANADIAN MUSEUM OF IMMIGRATION AT PIER 21

CHAPTER 5

A REFUGEE'S STORY: MARIANNE ECHT

ON A SNOWY DAY IN March 1939, Marianne Echt arrived at Pier 21 ready to embark on a new life. She spoke no English and knew no one outside her family. The Canadian government had seen potential in her father, who was both a pharmacist and a hobby farmer, and allowed them to immigrate. Marianne Echt knew she and her family were among the lucky ones when so many other Jewish families found the country's doors closed to them.

When Marianne was a young girl in the 1930s, she never dreamed that one day she would call Canada home. Her idyllic childhood was spent in Europe, in the resort town of Broesen. Marianne and her family were among the few Jews in the town of about four thousand people, not far from the Free City of Danzig (now called Gdańsk), a port city on the Baltic coast of Poland. The town had no synagogue, but the Echt family was often invited to special services held in the church or to parties held by their Christian neighbours.

When Marianne was not in her family's beautiful garden, she could be found playing at the nearby beach. "In the summer our friends and relatives from the city visited us every day, and we all went to the beach which was only a little way from our house. We used to take our lunch with us and stayed till evening or we went walking in the park," she wrote in a personal history that is now part of the collection at the Canadian Museum of Immigration at Pier 21.

Marianne (left) with her father and sister in Broesen. Marianne's father was a pharmacist, but he also ran a hobby farm. COURTESY OF THE CANADIAN MUSEUM OF IMMIGRATION AT PIER 21

Marianne's father, Otto, was a pharmacist. Connected to their home was a pharmacy and store that sold everything from fabrics to dishes. Aside from the family business, the Echts also had a small hobby farm that included a garden, chickens, and one cow.

NO LONGER SAFE

But this idyllic childhood soon came to an end. After Hitler became chancellor of Germany in 1933, Marianne, along with all the other Jews in the area, was no longer permitted to visit the beach or

THE FREE CITY

The Free City of Danzig existed between 1920 and 1939. It was made up of the port city, Danzig (now Gdańsk, Poland), and nearly two hundred towns in the surrounding areas. It was created after the First World War in accordance with the 1919 Treaty of Versailles.

The Free City, which included towns where mostly Germans lived, was under League of Nations protection. Poland was allowed to develop and maintain transportation and port facilities in the city in order to give the country access to a good seaport. While the city's population was primarily German, there were a significant number of Polish people living there too. The Germans living there resented being separated from Germany, and discriminated against the Polish. This resentment and discrimination grew stronger after 1933 when the Nazis took over the city's government. At this point many Jewish families fled.

After the Second World War, the city became part of Poland and the German population either left or was forced to return to Germany.

walk in the park. Marianne knew that her non-Jewish neighbours were mostly anti-Nazi and would never harm her family, but no one was safe from the hatred taking over the country, just outside their protected little town.

Before long, Hitler sent Nazis to Broesen. "These men came at night, broke the doors and windows of some of the people's houses, and brought the head of the family to a place which was unknown to all other people. The next day, the family of such persons would get a little gift. This gift consisted of a dainty, little parcel, mostly a box, wrapped in tissue paper and tied with a brightly colored ribbon. When it was opened, one found in the box the remains or ashes of the person of the family which had disappeared the night before. Also a little card was enclosed, a card of sympathy," Marianne wrote.

The terror escalated in Broesen. One day, the minister of the local parish returned home to find two halves of a dead cat on a gallows on his doorstep. A note that read, "Today the cat, tomorrow you," accompanied the gruesome sight. The minister also found his chicken coop had been robbed, with a note left behind: "God is everywhere, but not in the minister's chicken house."

KRISTALLNACHT

On November 9, 1938, Kristallnacht took place. That night, Nazi soldiers trashed the Echts' store, leaving the family and their customers terrified. A twelve-year-old girl at the time, Marianne remembers she was practising the piano when the Nazis came. She feared for her life. Marianne's parents knew they had only one choice left—leave Europe. "My father said, 'We're going to have to get out,'" Marianne remembered.

They applied for visas to Canada and were told the country was only accepting doctors and farmers. As both a pharmacist and a hobby farmer, Marianne's father qualified to become one of only about five thousand Jews given permission to enter Canada during Hitler's reigning years. Having come from East Prussia to Danzig, Marianne's father had a German passport, and she and her sisters were all listed on his document.

Marianne's stamped passport, 1939. COURTESY OF THE CANADIAN MUSEUM OF IMMIGRATION AT PIER 21

Since Marianne's father was deemed qualified to come to Canada, the Canadian government allowed her parents to apply for visas for the entire family: Marianne, her two younger sisters, and her maternal grandmother. Knowing that his money wasn't safe at home, Marianne's father had been keeping it in a bank in Poland. They

Marianne's immigration identification card, presented in Halifax. COURTESY OF THE CANADIAN MUSEUM OF IMMIGRATION AT PIER 21

would need it for their trip. After strip-searches, threats, and intensive questioning from local authorities, the Echts were finally able to leave Broesen. But saying goodbye to relatives, friends, and neighbours was heartbreaking. "Everyone asked us to take them with us, but that was impossible," Marianne wrote.

The Echts sold most of their personal belongings. What they didn't sell they packed and sent ahead of them to Gdynia, Poland. They stayed in Gdynia for ten days before sailing to England. Many of the family's closest friends were able to come at least this far with them to say goodbye, knowing they might never see them again.

SETTING SAIL FOR CANADA

On February 16, 1939, just three months before the *St. Louis* would sail from Hamburg on its doomed voyage, the Echts boarded a Polish ocean liner called the *Luvow* and sailed to England. After four days in England, they boarded the steamship *Andania*.

Advertisement for the Cunard Line's ship *Andania*, with service to Halifax.

The SS *Andania* was a British ocean liner launched in 1921. Built for the Cunard Line, the ship was 538 feet long and could carry more than 1,700 passengers and 270 crew members. When it was first launched, the SS *Andania* travelled mostly between Hamburg, Germany, and New York City, and later between Liverpool, England, and Montreal.

When the Second World War first broke out, the SS *Andania* was used as an armed merchant cruiser. In 1940, not long after the fighting began, the ship was torpedoed by a German submarine and badly damaged.

ARRIVING AT PIER 21

Of course, Marianne and her family had no idea of the SS *Andania*'s eventual fate when it arrived safely at Pier 21 on the Halifax

waterfront on March 7, 1939, less than one month after leaving England. Marianne remembers stepping off the ship on a stormy winter day, and into the cold, dingy pier. She was thirteen years old and spoke no English, but she didn't care about the weather or the pier's dismal appearance. She was happy to be in a country where she didn't have to be afraid to walk alone on the street.

At Pier 21, Sadie Fineberg from the Jewish Immigrant Aid Society welcomed the family. She brought them to a local boarding house where they stayed for a couple of months. The woman who ran the place spoke Yiddish, which made life easier for the Echts. After being introduced to several kind people in Halifax, Marianne's parents abandoned their plans to go to Montreal to start their new life. They decided to remain in Nova Scotia and look for a farm. "We had to come as farmers, although my father was actually a pharmacist," Marianne wrote.

Later that year, they bought a farm and settled in Milford Station, a picturesque area in Nova Scotia's Shubenacadie Valley, about a ninety-minute drive from Halifax. Marianne and her sisters attended a two-room schoolhouse, where they learned English quickly and made friends. They were happy for their newfound freedom, but life on the farm in rural Nova Scotia wasn't easy. Life was especially hard for Marianne's mother, Meta, who had grown accustomed to having a maid and had, for example, never baked bread before. Marianne's father couldn't afford hired help on the farm so he relied on his daughters to milk their forty cows and tend to the chickens, ducks, and turkeys. Marianne hated milking the cows before school.

A NEW, RURAL LIFE IN CANADA

Once the Echts were settled on their farm, Marianne, then sixteen years old, decided to write her memories of growing up in Broesen and her family's escape in a journal:

Marianne (centre) with her mother and sisters at their new home in Milford Station, Nova Scotia. COURTESY OF THE CANADIAN MUSEUM OF IMMIGRATION AT PIER 21

We bought the farm on which we live now and are much happier here than we were in Danzig. Of course, we work hard, but we have our freedom and that is better than living in a country of slavery. We do not wish to go back to Danzig because we like Canada very much. It is a land where all people have equal rights, where everybody may worship in his own way and where all people are free. May it always be so, and may no dictator ever set foot on Canadian soil.

While the family was grateful for their freedom, they couldn't forget the relatives they had left behind in war-torn Europe. They did everything they could to bring other family members to Canada. They promised to sponsor them so they wouldn't become burdens on the government, but they were refused. The Canadian government shut its doors to Jewish immigrants for the duration of the Second World War.

In 1946, Marianne and her family received a tragic, final letter from their relatives in Germany. The urgent letter, written from a park in Hamburg, explained that no more passenger ships were leaving Germany. The Echts never heard from them again. They later discovered the letter had been written just before their aunts, uncles, and cousins were picked up by the Gestapo and taken to Auschwitz, where they were executed.

Marianne, age sixteen, sat for this portrait in 1942. COURTESY OF THE CANADIAN MUSEUM OF IMMIGRATION AT PIER 21

For seven years Marianne's father worked the farm in Milford Station, leaving behind his former life as a pharmacist. Marianne lived on the farm until she started grade eleven, when her parents sent her to Halifax to live with family friends. They wanted her to attend a bigger school and get what they hoped would be a better education. Eventually, the whole family moved to Halifax and opened a corner store.

GIVING BACK

Touched by the generosity and caring they had received from Sadie Fineberg and the Jewish Immigrant Aid Society when they arrived at Pier 21, the Echts kept in contact with the Finebergs and developed a close relationship with the society. When Sadie

Marianne Ferguson (née Echt) on her wedding day in 1946. Marianne ended up marrying Lawrence Ferguson, a nephew of Sadie Fineberg's. COURTESY OF THE CANADIAN MUSEUM OF IMMIGRATION AT PIER 21

Marianne in Nova Scotia, 2004.

was appointed as a representative of Halifax's mayor, her position at the Jewish Immigrant Aid Society was left vacant. Marianne's mother soon stepped into the role. With her two younger sisters still in school, Marianne became her mother's helper at Pier 21. Marianne and her mother worked long hours in the immigration shed. Knowing what it was like to arrive vulnerable and alone in a new country, they spread kindness to the thousands of scared and tired refugees who came through.

In 1947, Canada began admitting Jewish war orphans and thousands of displaced people. Nearly two hundred and fifty thousand displaced persons (DPs) came to Canada between 1947 and 1962, and many had their journeys paid or partially paid for by the Canadian government. Watching the people arriving at Pier 21, Marianne couldn't help but look among them for the relatives she had left behind in Europe. She always left disappointed, but instead of losing herself in sadness or becoming bitter about her loss, she chose to show compassion and generosity toward the strangers she met. These strangers, she understood, had endured so much, not only surviving the war but also making it safely to Canada.

Marianne's connection to Pier 21 remained strong throughout her life. She eventually married, raised three children, and worked as a medical secretary at the IWK Health Centre and the QEII Health Sciences Centre in Halifax. But she never forgot

CANADA'S NATIONAL MUSEUMS

Canada has several national museums, most of which are based in Ottawa. The museums include the National Gallery of Canada and the Canadian Museum of Civilization.

The latter's collection of historical and cultural objects help Canadians understand and appreciate human cultural achievements and human behaviour. The Canadian Museum of Civilization includes the Canadian War Museum.

One permanent exhibit at the War Museum explores Canada's fight against dictatorships in Europe during the Second World War. The gallery tells visitors about the oppressive dictatorships of the 1930s, and the growing pressure for a strong military response from Canada and the rest of the world.

the valuable volunteer work she did after the war at Pier 21. When the Canadian Museum of Immigration at Pier 21 opened as the National Museum of Immigration in 1999, Marianne returned as a volunteer to guide visitors through the shed's history. She continues to serve as a living testament to the more than 1 million immigrants who passed through Pier 21 between 1928 and 1971.

Knowing she was one of the lucky ones to flee Nazi Germany in 1939 and find a home in Canada, Marianne is grateful. But when reflecting on the years leading up to the Second World War and her stolen childhood, she says she is reminded of Henry Wadsworth Longfellow's poem "My Lost Youth":

> There are things of which I may not speak;
> There are dreams that cannot die;
> There are thoughts that make the strong heart weak,
> And bring a pallor into the cheek,
> And a mist before the eye.

"To me," Marianne wrote, "those words mean that I have seen and experienced so much during my childhood in Danzig; the things

Mr. and Mrs. Lawrence Ferguson in Halifax c. 1998. COURTESY OF THE CANADIAN MUSEUM OF IMMIGRATION AT PIER 21

are hard to speak of, but the memory cannot die, and yet, it makes me sad to think of them.

"And even in such a country, a country of tyranny, barbarism and hatred, people have dreams of freedom, which may come true to some of them but may not come to others. Like a sunbeam from a clouded sky, came a permission for us to come to Canada, a free country."

A German anti-Semitic propaganda poster that reads, "Behind enemy powers: the Jew," c. 1933–39. COURTESY OF THE UNITED STATES HOLOCAUST MEMORIAL MUSEUM

CHAPTER 6

CANADIAN IMMIGRATION POLICIES

ON MAY 5, 1945, GERMAN forces in northwest Europe surrendered. Hitler had committed suicide just days before on April 30, and although the fighting was not yet over—the war with Japan was still underway and would not end until September 1945—the major threat of Nazi Germany had ended. Victory in Europe, or VE Day, was officially celebrated three days later, on May 8, 1945.

In Germany, where the Canadian Army fought to the last day, soldiers were too tired and relieved to celebrate much on VE Day. But in Paris and London, Canadians joined thousands of public celebrators in an outpouring of emotion. In Toronto, people danced in the streets.

The war was officially over, but anti-Semitic sentiments had hardly dissipated and many people still believed the Nazi propaganda about Jews being responsible for the war. When asked by journalists in an off-the-record conversation about how many Jews would be allowed into Canada now that the war in Europe was over, one anonymous senior official uttered four telling words that reflected the prevailing view of people across the country: "None is too many."

During the spring of 1945, Allied forces liberated concentration camps throughout Nazi-occupied Europe and the full extent of the Holocaust was brought to light. German soldiers and their collaborators had killed nearly two out of every three European Jews. The killings were part of what became known as "The Final Solution," the Nazi plan to murder all the Jews in Europe.

DISPLACED PERSONS

After the war, many of the survivors of the Holocaust and its death camps found safety and shelter in displaced persons (DP) camps run by the Allied forces. Displaced persons were somewhat different from refugees. They were defined as people who had been forced to leave their country and were part of a phenomenon known as "forced migration." Unable to return to their former homes, they stayed in the camps until they could find new homes. Thousands eventually immigrated to the State of Israel, which was established in May 1948, and by 1953 as many as one hundred and seventy thousand Jewish displaced persons and refugees had immigrated to that country. Other Jewish DPs immigrated to countries like the United States and Canada.

After seeing the images of concentration camp survivors waiting in DP camps, unable to return to their homes due to the trauma they had suffered and the anti-Semitism that still existed, Canadians were moved. They began to re-evaluate their country's discriminatory immigration policies, and became more willing to accept a significant number of displaced persons.

This was a change from the war years. While the Canadian government welcomed more than six thousand British women and child war evacuees to Canada in 1939 (and, in 1944, discharged UK service personnel and their dependants without restriction), the country delayed or rejected thousands of requests from Jewish refugees. Between 1939 and 1945 more than forty thousand British nationals, more than thirty thousand American citizens, and fifteen thousand nationals from other countries were admitted to Canada. Approximately five thousand Jews were admitted between 1933 and 1945.

Prisoners at Auschwitz concentration camp celebrate as Allied forces finally liberate them in 1945. COURTESY OF THE UNITED STATES HOLOCAUST MEMORIAL MUSEUM

Canada's record for accepting Jewish immigrants would improve slightly in the years after the war. By the summer of 1948, Canada had approved or admitted more than one hundred and eighty thousand postwar immigrants, including sixty-five thousand displaced persons. Among the displaced persons were eight thousand Jews. In the same year, Canada created a new immigration act, under which immigration continued to grow. For the next few years the numbers of Jews admitted to Canada would be larger than at almost any other time in Canadian history.

Clarence Decatur (C. D.) Howe, minister in charge of Canada's Department of Reconstruction and Supply, had pushed his colleagues for a more effective immigration policy. His arguments were based not on humanitarian grounds, but on the fact that the country simply needed more workers after the war. Without new immigrants, he

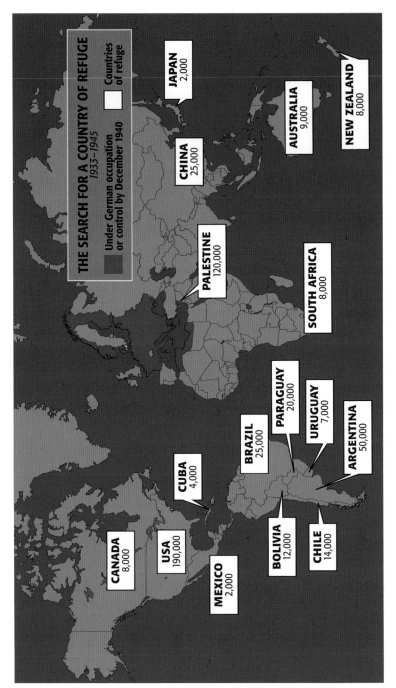

THE SEARCH FOR A COUNTRY OF REFUGE
1933–1945

Under German occupation
or control by December 1940

Countries
of refuge

JAPAN
2,000

CHINA
25,000

AUSTRALIA
9,000

NEW ZEALAND
8,000

PALESTINE
120,000

SOUTH AFRICA
8,000

PARAGUAY
20,000

URUGUAY
7,000

ARGENTINA
50,000

BRAZIL
25,000

CUBA
4,000

BOLIVIA
12,000

CHILE
14,000

CANADA
8,000

USA
190,000

MEXICO
2,000

A map of the world showing how many Jewish refugees were accepted and by which countries between 1933 and 1945.

argued, Canada would face severe labour shortages. Howe's concerns were heard. On May 1, 1947, Prime Minister Mackenzie King rose in the House of Commons to speak about Canada's immigration policy and set out a new long-term commitment to sustain population growth and thus aid the country's economic development. But to understand the way forward, we must look to our past.

IMMIGRATION IN CANADA'S EARLY DAYS

For most of its history, Canada not only welcomed, but actively encouraged immigration. In the early days, the immigrants who settled in Canada came mostly from Great Britain and Europe. They came in search of greater economic opportunities and with hopes of building new lives for themselves and their families.

When Canada was founded in 1867, it built its immigration policies on the belief that expanding the country's population was essential to filling the vast land in the west, producing agricultural products to sell, and supplying the inexpensive labour force that was needed for industrialization. For Canada to survive as an independent, prosperous nation, and to continue to grow economically, it needed a larger population and an expanding market. During the first three decades following Confederation, there were few obstacles in the way of newcomers settling in Canada.

Canada's population rapidly grew at the turn of the century. Between 1896 and 1914, more than 3 million immigrants settled here. In the decade between 1901 and 1911, the Canadian population jumped by 43 percent. The percentage of people living in Canada who were born outside the country grew to more than 22 percent. Immigration from Great Britain, the US, Europe, and Asia transformed the country, particularly western Canada.

Amendments to Canada's Immigration Act in 1906 and 1910 allowed the government to be more selective about who was allowed to enter. Prime Minister Wilfrid Laurier's cabinet was given

enhanced powers to exclude any group of immigrants if it was seen to be in the best interests of the country. Restrictive regulations were placed, for example, on the admission of Chinese immigrants by way of head taxes, and quotas were set on Japanese immigration. The number of Asian immigrants drastically declined due to these restrictions.

Canada's first choice was clearly European immigrants, but slowly became more willing to accept those from Eastern European countries as well. In September 1925, Ottawa signed an agreement with the Canadian Pacific Railway (CPR) and the Canadian National Railway (CNR) giving them control over recruiting European agriculturalists. The agreement was part of the government's efforts to fulfill Canada's growing labour needs. Industrialists, farmers, and transportation companies argued the country needed more workers and lobbied the government for a more liberal immigration policy. The railways were also allowed to recruit immigrants from countries that had previously been designated as "non-preferred" by the Department of Immigration and Colonization. Prospective immigrants from countries like Estonia, Latvia, Lithuania, Poland, Russia, Hungary, Czechoslovakia, Austria, and Germany were now allowed to enter Canada.

But that ended with the Great Depression, when immigration to Canada was essentially halted. In August 1930, the federal government passed an Order-in-Council that suspended immigration from Europe, except for those who had enough money to buy a farm and live self-sufficiently in Canada. This move was followed by the notorious Order-in-Council PC 695, which permitted only British subjects and American citizens with sufficient savings to support themselves until they found a job, farmers with enough money to farm in Canada, farm labourers with guaranteed employment, and people who had jobs in the mining, lumbering, or logging industries. Immigration dropped to one hundred and forty thousand people between 1931 and 1941, down from close to 1.2 million people in the decade between 1921 and 1931.

IMMIGRATION LEGISLATION

Order-in-Council PC 695 was passed on March 21, 1931, and was the most limiting policy to date in Canada. The legislation restricted immigration to: British and American citizens with sufficient means to support themselves until they found permanent jobs; agriculturalists who could farm the land; and wives or minors of Canadian residents. Everyone else was prohibited.

The party line of Prime Minister R. B. Bennett's conservative government was that the restrictions were necessary to prevent widespread unemployment and general economic decline.

In 1939, it was this policy that was cited when Canadians called for amnesty for the Jewish refugees aboard the MS *St. Louis*. Government authorities staunchly opposed their admission and in so doing, ostensibly sent over 250 people to their deaths in Nazi-occupied Europe.

Under the new agreement, the railway companies could issue occupational certificates to immigrants from countries that had previously been dubbed "non-preferred." This led to a large number of foreign labourers from Eastern European countries such as Latvia, Lithuania, Poland, Russia, Yugoslavia, and Germany.

The railways were told not to accept Jewish farmers because the government believed Jews were not genuine farmers and would likely move to the city. Immigrants who failed to settle the land or find farm employment within one year could be deported.

Between 1925 and 1929, more than 185,000 Europeans arrived under the agreement. The agreement was cancelled in 1930, due in part to a change in government, widespread unemployment, and general economic instability.

WELCOMING REFUGEES

A small percentage of those who come to Canada—like the Jews before and after the Second World War—do so to escape horrible political and social conditions in their homelands. They are forced

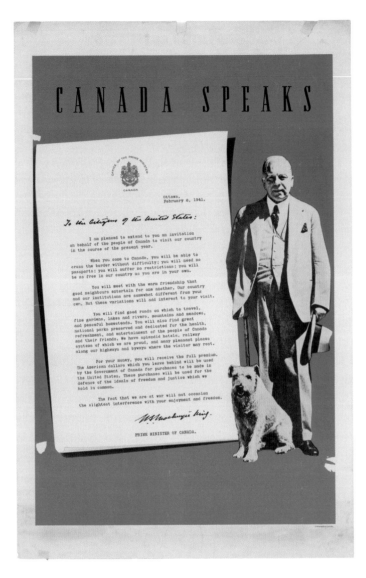

A promotional poster from Prime Minister King "to the citizens of the United States" highlighting the stark contrast between his attitude toward Jewish refugees and American patriots: "Cross the border without difficulty; you will need no passport; you will suffer no restrictions." LIBRARY AND ARCHIVES CANADA

to flee because of threats of persecution and because they lack protection in their own country. The decision to become a refugee usually has its roots in racial, religious, or ideological beliefs, which separate the refugee from the majority of others in his or her country. How much Canada has helped refugees, by allowing them to settle here, has largely depended on the political and economic conditions in Canada at the time.

When Canada had the opportunity to show compassion during the 1930s and 1940s, it chose to shut itself off from the rest of world and fought attempts by desperate Jewish refugees to break through the government's restrictive legislation of March 1931.

Refugees who were successful in overcoming Canada's tough immigration rules during the 1930s usually had money and marketable job skills. Thomas Bata, the Czech-born industrialist and head of the Bata shoemaking empire, is one famous example. Refugees like Bata, who moved his family business to Canada ahead of the German invasion of Czechoslovakia, were a real boost to the Canadian economy. According to a Canadian senate standing committee on immigration and labour brief presented by the CNCR in 1946, refugees are estimated to have started dozens of industries in Canada between 1939 and 1942, producing goods valued at more than $22 million and employing close to five thousand people.

In 1938, before the start of the Second World War, President Roosevelt pushed to create an international agency called the Intergovernmental Committee on Refugees (IGCR or ICR). Its purpose was to resettle refugees from Nazi Germany and to prepare for the resettlement of future German immigrants. The agency was the beginning of planned resettlement of refugees. At the agency's founding meeting, the committee's thirty-two states defined refugees as: "Persons possessing, or having possessed, German nationality and who are not professing any other nationality and who are proved not to otherwise enjoy, either in practice or in law, the protection of the German government." In 1943, the I(G)CR's mandate was expanded to cover all European refugees.

By 1950, the chief international intergovernmental organization providing legal protection and care to refugees was the Office of the High Commissioner for Refugees, established by the United Nations General Assembly. The most widely accepted definition of a refugee today still remains as stated in the 1951 Convention Relating to the Status of Refugees. The convention is the key legal document defining refugees, their rights, and the legal obligations of countries in which they live.

POSTWAR REFUGEES

In the years following the Second World War, Canada became one of the first countries in the world to admit refugees. Nearly two hundred and fifty thousand displaced persons came to Canada between 1947 and 1962.

New Canadian postwar immigration laws stated that no one could be excluded from the country because of their race, religion, or place of birth. These were different from the previous laws, which had discriminated against people of certain races or from particular countries. Education, training, and skills formed the new basis for being allowed entry into Canada. People would now be admitted based on their ability to contribute to the country's economy. The new laws led to a significant increase in immigration to Canada.

Continuing through the 1960s and 1970s, increasing numbers of Canadians wanted an immigration policy that reflected their desire to have a racially inclusive country. They wanted to see more people from countries around the world allowed to become residents of Canada. The government responded. By the early 1970s, people from Asia and other non-European countries made up more than half of all immigrants to Canada.

UNHCR

In 1951, the Office of the United Nations High Commissioner for Refugees (UNHCR) was established by the United Nations General Assembly to help Europeans displaced by the Second World War. Initially, it was given an optimistic three-year mandate to complete its work and then dissolve. But the job of leading and co-ordinating international action to protect refugees and resolve refugee problems around the world turned out to be essential in the long term.

In 1954, the new organization won the Nobel Peace Prize for its work in helping the refugees of Europe. Two years later, the UNHCR faced a major emergency: refugees poured out of Hungary after Soviet forces crushed the Hungarian Revolution.

The agency's primary purpose continues to be protecting the rights and well-being of refugees. Today, the agency is made up of more than 9,300 people in 123 countries, and helps millions of vulnerable refugees.

THE BOAT PEOPLE

When the Vietnam War ended in 1975, one million Vietnamese people fled their homes looking for refuge and freedom. Many tried escaping across the South China Sea in small, unsafe boats. These refugees, known as "the boat people," became an international humanitarian crisis as the surrounding countries in Southeast Asia were overwhelmed and grew increasingly unwilling to accept them.

Canada responded by opening its doors to the refugees from Vietnam, Cambodia, and Laos. In 1979, Prime Minister Joe Clark announced that the Canadian government would admit fifty thousand refugees. In response to dramatic media reports showing the boat people leaving their homeland in desperation and risking their lives, thousands of Canadians came forward wanting to help. Public pressure forced the government to increase the number of refugees it had initially agreed to accept to sixty thousand.

The Canadian government decided that the number of boat people brought to Canada should be dependent on public support.

In July 1979, it introduced a matching formula: the government would sponsor one refugee for each one sponsored by ordinary Canadians or private organizations. Churches, corporations, and groups of five or more adult Canadian citizens were eligible to sponsor refugees directly.

Between 1975 and 1976, Canada admitted just under six thousand Vietnamese immigrants. Another fifty thousand joined them in a second wave, mostly between 1979 and 1980.

CANADA'S NEW IMMIGRATION ACT

A new Canadian Immigration Act went into effect in 1978. It contained Canada's first formal policy on the status of refugees. For the first time, the act made it possible for refugees to apply for admission as immigrants. It also set out specific goals for re-uniting families, being fair to immigrants of all races, providing safety to refugees, and helping newcomers adjust to life in Canada. Between 1978 and 1981, refugees made up about 25 percent of all immigrants to Canada, many of them coming from Southeast Asia.

Canada continued its more open-door immigration policy through the 1980s and early 1990s, despite severe economic recessions. The country's efforts were recognized in 1986 when the United Nations High Commissioner for Refugees (UNHCR) awarded the Nansen Refugee Award to "the people of Canada." Canada had taken in more than one hundred and fifty thousand refugees in the previous decade. It was the first time the medal had been awarded to a group, let alone to an entire country.

In 1990, the government of Prime Minister Brian Mulroney unveiled its "Five Year Plan for Immigration," proposing an increase in total immigration to two hundred and fifty thousand in 1992, up from two hundred thousand in 1990. The long-term commitment to planned immigration was new in Canadian history, as was the proposal to increase immigration at a time of economic recession.

THE NANSEN REFUGEE AWARD

Awarded annually, the UNHCR Nansen Refugee Award honours extraordinary service—by a person or organization—to forced migrants. The award is named for Norwegian Fridtjof Nansen, the first High Commissioner for Refugees for the League of Nations.

Each year at a stately ceremony in Geneva, Switzerland, the honouree is presented with a commemorative medal and a $100,000 USD cash prize to fund their efforts.

Established in 1954, the list of laureates is long and varied. The inaugural prize was awarded to Eleanor Roosevelt for her lifetime dedication to refugees and humanitarian aid. Since then, the laureates have included the International Red Cross (1957); Juan Carlos I (1987), the former king of Spain; and Médecins Sans Frontières/ Doctors Without Borders (1993), among others.

In 1986, "the people of Canada" received the Nansen Award, and then-Governor General Jeanne Sauvé accepted the prize on behalf of the country. It was the first—and only—time the UNHCR had recognized an entire country for its commitment to refugees. Brian Mulroney was Canada's prime minister at the time.

KOSOVAR REFUGEES

In the spring of 1999, Canada was called upon to help Kosovar refugees living in camps in Macedonia following the Kosovo War. The United Nations High Commissioner for Refugees asked a number of countries to provide safe haven for the refugees after an estimated three hundred and fifty thousand people fled Kosovo in the span of just eleven days. Canada responded immediately with

an offer to accept five thousand people. In addition, more than two thousand refugees were admitted to Canada under the Family Reunification and Special Needs programs, which remained in effect after the evacuation of the Kosovar refugees.

While Canadians responded with open arms to the Kosovar refugees, the response was the polar opposite a few months later when a boat carrying 123 Chinese passengers arrived off the west coast in July 1999. The public response was largely hostile because the Chinese migrants had tried to enter Canada illegally. Throughout the summer of 1999, nearly 600 people arrived on the coast of British Columbia in four decrepit boats and one shipping container, having paid smugglers large sums of money to escape the impoverished Fujian province in China. They hadn't applied to enter Canada as immigrants and didn't qualify as refugees. Canadian officials declared them illegal immigrants and jailed them until officials decided what to do next. Most were eventually sent back to China.

As their refugee claims and appeals dragged on, many of the Chinese "illegals" spent months in a Canadian jail and for a few it was as long as two years. A United Nations human rights review of the treatment of those migrants criticized Canadian authorities for handcuffing and incarcerating them like criminals "for having committed no crime but that of being deceived [by human traffickers]."

TAMIL MIGRANTS

More than a decade later, in August 2010, the rundown cargo ship MV (motor vessel) *Sun Sea* arrived in British Columbia carrying nearly five hundred Tamil migrants from Sri Lanka seeking asylum. The ship was not warmly welcomed. The men, women, and children from Southeast Asia were detained in a provincial prison for months. The ship's arrival had Canadian officials worried about

HUMAN TRAFFICKING

Human trafficking has been called a modern-day form of slavery because it involves the illegal trade of people, often for money. It is not only illegal, but also a violation of human rights.

Every year, millions of men, women, and even children are trafficked in countries around the world, including Canada. Human trafficking is believed to generate billions of dollars of profit every year.

In Canada, the victims of human trafficking rarely go to police to get help because they fear the traffickers, and often don't speak English or French. Traffickers use physical force, fraud, or coercion to force their victims into work. Often they are forced into illegal work like prostitution.

Similar to human trafficking, human smuggling is illegal. It happens when people are brought into a country, like Canada, by deliberately evading immigration laws. People will voluntarily pay a smuggler in order to gain illegal entry into a country. Unlike human smuggling, the victims of human trafficking are often tricked or forced into entering another country.

several things: people arriving illegally on Canadian shores, the dangers of human smuggling, and the possibility that some of the migrants were affiliated with the Tamil Tigers. The political and military group had been fighting for an independent homeland in Sri Lanka since the 1970s, and Canada considered it a terrorist organization.

"Canadian officials will look at all available options to strengthen our laws in order to address this unacceptable abuse of international law and Canadian generosity," Vic Toews, Canada's public safety minister, said in a statement on the arrival of the *Sun Sea*.

Throughout the 1990s and early 2000s, Canada had one of the highest immigration rates in the industrialized world. Between 1995 and 2008, about two hundred and forty thousand people immigrated to Canada every year. But it was clear Canada would

only accept immigrants or refugees who entered the country by following its rules. The message was that those who tried to enter illegally would be punished and sent home.

CHANGES TO CANADA'S IMMIGRATION LAWS

Immigration laws in Canada and around the world were tightened following the terrorist attacks of September 11, 2001, on the World Trade Center and the Pentagon in the United States. Canada enacted the Immigration and Refugee Protection Act in 2002. While the act was influenced by heightened concerns for the country's security, much of the legislation had been drafted long before September 11. The 2002 legislation made it clear that potential immigrants or refugees could not be excluded on the basis of race. The legislation also focused on helping to protect refugees and helping families reunite.

By continually holding the government to account, average Canadians carry on shaping the country's immigration policy. Values such as freedom, respect for cultural differences, and a commitment to social justice are promoted in the Canadian Charter of Rights and Freedoms, and influence who is considered an "ideal immigrant." As in all democratic countries, Canadians collectively decide whether the same criteria or standards apply to everyone who wants to enter the country or whether they should change depending on the person or situation. Which potential immigrants may *not* legitimately be allowed to enter the country is also decided. In Canada, for example, known terrorists are not welcomed.

In 2015, with Europe confronting its worst refugee crisis since the Second World War, Canada was once again been called upon to take action and re-examine some of these questions. The United Nations has urged a global response to end the civil war in Syria,

which began in 2011 with pro-democracy, anti-government protests against President Bashar al-Assad, and escalated into a full-blown civil war. The conflict has since sent millions of people fleeing from their homes.

According to the United Nations, 6.5 million Syrians are internally displaced and more than 4.6 million have sought refuge in the neighbouring countries of Egypt, Iraq, Jordan, Lebanon, Turkey, and in Europe. Canada responded by providing close to $1 billion in humanitarian, development, and security assistance to provide food, shelter, and health care to Syrians affected by the crisis. In 2015, Prime Minister Justin Trudeau committed to bring 25,000 Syrian refugees to Canada by the end of February 2016.

CHAPTER 7

LASTING LESSONS

"Had Canada taken a stand, had it been true to its best and highest values, had it opened its doors of refuge to those passengers fleeing the violent anti-Semitism of the Nazi regime, it is probable that those six hundred and twenty children, women and men [remaining passengers on the St. Louis] would have walked down the gangplank right here and passed through these halls, following with some...million others...who came through this place seeking the promise of Canada's freedom and peace. In creating this permanent memorial, we are remembering the harrowing plight of the Voyage of the Damned. We are remembering both those who were consumed by the Holocaust, as well as those who survived it."

—JASON KENNEY, MINISTER OF CITIZENSHIP, IMMIGRATION, AND MULTICULTURALISM, AT THE *WHEEL OF CONSCIENCE* UNVEILING CEREMONY, 2011

AFTER THE WAR, WHEN IMMIGRATION to Canada resumed on a large scale, Pier 21 became one of three national gateways to Canada. Hundreds of thousands of immigrants entered the country through its doors. In the years immediately after the war, it is estimated that of the five hundred thousand immigrants who came to Canada, about one hundred thousand were displaced persons or refugees, like those aboard the *St. Louis*. Large numbers of displaced people did not begin arriving in Canada until 1947—two years after the war had ended. Postwar immigration to Canada peaked in 1957 with the arrival of 282,000 immigrants that year. Of those people, 73,627—over a quarter—passed through Halifax.

(opposite) Author Art Spiegelman (*Maus*) created this full-page editorial for the *Washington Post* on the seventieth anniversary of the *St. Louis*'s voyage.

WHAT HAPPENED TO THE MS *ST. LOUIS*?

After the *St. Louis* stopped bringing leisure passengers to Halifax in 1939, it was used for war purposes. Until 1944, it served as a German naval accommodation ship—temporary barracks for sailors. On August 30, 1944, it was badly damaged in Kiel, Germany, during bombings by the Allied forces. The ship was partially restored, and by 1946 the MS *St. Louis* was being used as a floating hotel in Hamburg, though it was never fully repaired. Six years later, the ship was broken up and its pieces were sold for scrap.

After transatlantic flight became more prevalent in the late 1950s, fewer ships arrived at Pier 21. Eventually the doors of the Pier 21 immigration shed closed for good on March 28, 1971—forty-three years after they were first opened and one million people had passed through. The Canadian Museum of Immigration at Pier 21 opened as a national museum on July 1, Canada Day, 1999.

Seventy-two years after the fateful voyage of the MS *St. Louis*, in 2011, a memorial to the ship's Jewish passengers was unveiled in Halifax at the Canadian Museum of Immigration at Pier 21, the place where the ship would have docked if the Canadian government had granted permission.

The Wheel of Conscience is the $500,000 steel memorial designed by renowned architect Daniel Libeskind, who was born in Poland and is the son of Holocaust survivors. It was developed through a partnership between the Canadian Jewish Congress and Citizenship and Immigration Canada to commemorate the story of the *St. Louis*.

In the end, more than one-third of the refugees onboard the *St. Louis* who returned to Europe died under Hitler's campaign to rid Germany and the world of Jews. Had Canada or the United States relaxed their immigration rules at the time, those deaths could have been prevented.

One of the important questions the *St. Louis* raised for Canadians was: Is it ever okay for a country to overlook its immigration policy? If Canada had temporarily set aside its immigration regulations in 1939 in order to accommodate the Jewish refugees aboard the *St. Louis,* would that have set a dangerous precedent, or would relaxing the regulations have been the correct, humanitarian decision?

Since the end of the Second World War, Canada has had a long history of welcoming refugees, from the thousands of Hungarians who came after the collapse of the 1956 uprising against Soviet rule, to the Kosovar refugees seeking a safe haven following armed conflict in 1999. But the darker times in Canada's history can't be forgotten. The *St. Louis* was one of them. "We dedicate ourselves to teaching future generations about the injustices and xenophobia of our own history, and to ensuring that they are never repeated," Jason Kenney, minister of Citizenship, Immigration, and Multiculturalism, said in 2011.

> *"Xenophobia is an unreasonable fear or hatred of foreigners, strangers, or anything that is foreign or strange."*
>
> —JASON KENNEY, 2011

Today's Canada is different from that of 1939. The country has become more tolerant and culturally diverse, but there is still much progress to be made. Thinking about the *St. Louis* and facing the sad moments in Canada's history is important; it helps Canadians learn from the past and move forward as a nation to make informed decisions for a better future—a future that sees Canada implement policies that will allow it to stand out as a country of refuge and a beacon for those legitimately facing persecution by their governments.

SEEKING REPENTANCE

Part of the process of moving forward is saying sorry and having the apology accepted. But for sins of the past, who issues the apology for a nation's mistakes? In 2000, survivors of the *St. Louis* were invited to a dinner in Ottawa held by Christian leaders who wanted to apologize for Canada's behaviour toward the Jewish refugees in 1939.

Among the Christians present was Douglas Blair, a Baptist minister from Sarnia, Ontario. He is the great-nephew of Frederick Blair, the minister of immigration whom Prime Minister Mackenzie King had empowered to decide the fate of the *St. Louis* passengers. Douglas had never met his distant relative, but said he was shocked at the central role his great-uncle had played. He said he felt the need to atone and repent for Frederick's sins.

"I have come to beg your forgiveness for the deep, deep wrong that was done to you. I understand very well that my name is not one dear to your heart," Blair said to the twenty-five survivors present. "Will you forgive me and let me call you my friends?"

Following his speech, some of the surviving passengers of the *St. Louis* embraced him. "This is the most unusual thing that's ever happened. No one so far has ever come forward, of the many countries who just closed their doors on us, and has come to say they're sorry and to apologize. And this is historic," one of the passengers who met with Blair said, summing up the feelings of the other survivors.

Blair and the other Christians at the meeting said Canada's churches had sinned in two ways: first by ignoring the pleas for support of those Canadians who wanted King to loosen the restrictions on Jewish immigration or make an exception in order to accommodate the *St. Louis*'s Jewish refugees; and second by agreeing with the actions of church members who used anti-Semitic lies to argue against granting asylum to the Jewish refugees.

The suitcase carried by sixteen-year-old Annaeliese Weil when she emigrated to the United States on the MS *St. Louis* in 1938, one year before its ill-fated voyage. COURTESY OF THE UNITED STATES HOLOCAUST MEMORIAL MUSEUM

One of the Jewish survivors of the *St. Louis* said that he might be able to forgive Canada's churches for what occurred in the past. But, he said, he "reserved the right not to forget." The meeting called into question whether the small group of survivors of the *St. Louis* could accept an apology and grant forgiveness on behalf of the more than 250 passengers of the ship who ultimately died in the Holocaust—and whether there is ever a point when it is too late to ask for forgiveness and too late to grant it.

On June 6, 2009, the US Senate passed Resolution 111, recognizing the seventieth anniversary of the voyage of the *St. Louis*. The resolution honoured the memory of all those onboard and recognized the anniversary as an opportunity for "public officials and educators to raise awareness about an important historical event, the lessons of which are relevant to current and future generations." Pulitzer Prize–winning author Art Spiegelman (*Maus*) even illustrated a full-page editorial cartoon for the *Washington Post* (see page 102) to commemorate the whole affair.

MEMORIALIZING A TRAGEDY

The Wheel of Conscience at the Canadian Immigration Museum at Pier 21 in Halifax is just one of the many memorials and artistic tributes made to the MS *St. Louis*'s tragic voyage. In his artist

The kinetic installation by Daniel Libeskind at the Canadian Museum of Immigration at Pier 21 in Halifax, Nova Scotia, once one of the "gateways to Canada" for millions of European immigrants. COURTESY OF THE CANADIAN MUSEUM OF IMMIGRATION AT PIER 21

statement, *Wheel of Conscience* designer Daniel Libeskind, an internationally recognized architect, described the heavy, polished stainless steel wheel as driven by gears, which are symbolic of both the gears of a ship and the gears of government. The words *hatred, racism,* and *xenophobia* appear on three gears from smallest to largest. The gears move the largest and most prominent wheel, labelled *anti-Semitism.*

The smallest and fastest rotating gear, marked *hatred*, moves first. Its force is then transferred to the next larger gear, *racism*. Then, the force of *hatred* and *racism* turn the larger gear of *xeno-phobia*. Finally, all three gears are engaged and move the higher gear of *anti-Semitism*.

As one gear turns the next, they slowly disassemble and repro-duce an image of the *St. Louis*. The interdependent gears are meant to represent the vicious cycle that brought tragedy and dishonour to Canada in 1939. Around the edge of the facing side of the monu-ment is the story of the ship's fateful voyage and on the reverse is a complete passenger list. The memorial implores Canadians to never again let the country fail such a test of humanity.

"What brilliant symbolism: the very facility through which these refugees could have entered and found refuge only to have the door slammed in their face will now feature an enduring memorial to their memory," Mr. Libeskind wrote in a piece he published in the *Ottawa Citizen* newspaper in the fall of 2010.

As a way of exploring the Canadian connection to this tragic voyage, the Maritime Museum of the Atlantic in Halifax devel-oped a travelling exhibit in 2009 called *St. Louis: Ship of Fate*. Through first-hand testimonials, photographs, and interactive features, the exhibit strives to create broader awareness about the tragic story of war and national policy.

In Washington, DC, the United States Holocaust Memorial Museum created a permanent exhibit that tells the detailed story of the voyage of the *St. Louis*. The museum also published a thor-oughly researched book, *Refuge Denied: The St. Louis Passengers and the Holocaust*, written by Sarah A. Ogilvie and Scott Miller. Although the episode of the *St. Louis* was well known at the time of the book's publication in 2006, the actual fates of the passengers, once they disembarked, were largely unknown. Through a decade of research, the writers uncovered what happened to each of the 937 refugees onboard the ship.

MOVING FORWARD

Canada can take pride in the country's actions in the years following the end of the Second World War. The country welcomed about forty thousand Holocaust survivors during the late 1940s and lived up to its highest values by becoming the third-largest refuge in the world for survivors, behind Israel and the United States.

Canada's immigration policies continue to evolve in response to the needs of people around the world, including refugees who, like the Jews before and after the war, are in need of safety. In the last twenty-five years more than 3 million people have arrived in Canada to begin new lives. About two hundred thousand immigrants arrive each year, and of those, about twenty thousand are refugees.

Today, people from more than two hundred ethnic groups call Canada home, making the country a patchwork of different cultures. If Canadians were to stand as a group they would resemble a colourful mosaic made of small pieces of differently coloured glass or stone set together. Through immigration, Canada has become a wonderfully diverse place. Most Canadians are in fact immigrants, or the descendants of immigrants.

Nevertheless, racism has been a sad part of Canada's past, especially in its relationship to Aboriginal people, and continues to persist today. Each year, our provincial and federal governments continue work to make amends for historical wrongs. In 2015, for example, the country's Truth and Reconciliation Commission

CHECK IT OUT ONLINE

Canada's current immigration policy: cic.gc.ca

United States Holocaust Memorial Museum: ushmm.org

Canadian Museum of Immigration at Pier 21: pier21.ca

released a landmark report. The report included ninety-four rec-ommendations or "calls to action" for change in government poli-cies and programs to repair the relationship between Aboriginal people and the federal and provincial governments of Canada. The commission's work and the calls to action were seen as important steps in the healing process and to making amends. Confronting the past and learning about the horrific mistakes is one way to curb racism and the harmful beliefs that lead to racist immigra-tion policies.

Around the world, Canada is primarily seen as a fair country where people are considered equal under the law regardless of their religion, skin colour, or first language. Canada does not have a his-tory of civil war or the widespread violence found in many other countries. It is seen as a country that allows people to make a new start in a new place. As a country largely made up of immigrants, it not only makes sense, but is appropriate that Canada, going into the future, have an immigration policy that is among the fairest and most welcoming in the world.

ACKNOWLEDGEMENTS

First, I would like to say thank you to everyone at Nimbus Publishing, in particular Patrick Murphy, Whitney Moran, Kate Kennedy, and especially Emily MacKinnon for her thoughtful and thorough editing. Special thanks to designer Jenn Embree for making the final product look so good.

My gratitude to all those who wrote about the *St. Louis* before me, especially Sarah A. Ogilvie and Scott Miller, authors of the book *Refuge Denied: The St. Louis Passengers and the Holocaust*. Their research and insight were invaluable.

Thanks are also due to the United States Holocaust Memorial Museum, Library and Archives Canada, the Canadian Museum of Immigration at Pier 21, the Maritime Museum of the Atlantic, Nova Scotia Archives, Dalhousie University, and the Halifax Public Libraries for their wonderful collections of books, newspapers, photographs, and other materials. Thanks also to Rafael Medoff, director of the David S. Wyman Institute for Holocaust Studies, for his insight.

Finally, my deepest thank you to my family—Robbie, Natasha, and Lara, who are always there for me with love—and to my extended family and friends who help me along my way.

BIBLIOGRAPHY

In addition to the books and websites listed below, the following newspapers, c. 1900–2014, provided valuable research material: *Halifax Chronicle, Halifax Herald,* the *Chronicle-Herald,* the *Globe and Mail,* and the *National Post.*

Abella, Irving, and Harold Troper. *None is Too Many.* New York: Random House, 1982.

Carlson, Kathryn Blaze. "'None is Too Many': Memorial for Jews turned away from Canada in 1939," *Globe and Mail.* January 17, 2011.

Dench, Janet. *A Hundred Years of Immigration to Canada 1900-1999: A Chronology Focusing on Refugees and Discrimination.* The Canadian Council for Refugees.

Dicks, Gerald E. *Canada's Refugee Policy: Indifference or Opportunism?* Montreal: McGill-Queen's University Press, 1977.

Duivenvoorden-Mitic, Trudy, and J. P. LeBlanc. *Pier 21: The Gateway That Changed Canada.* Halifax: Nimbus Publishing, 1988.

Frost, James. *Canada's Atlantic Gateway: An Illustrated History of the Port of Halifax.* Halifax: Nimbus Publishing, 2008.

Granfield, Linda. *Pier 21: Gateway of Hope.* Toronto: Tundra Books, 2000.

Henderson, Jennifer, and Pauline Wakeham. *Reconciling Canada: Critical Perspectives on the Culture of Redress.* Toronto: University of Toronto Press, 2013.

Hodge, Deborah. *Kids Book of Canadian Immigration.* Toronto: Kids Can Press, 2006.

Kacer, Kathy. *To Hope and Back: The Journey of the St. Louis.* Toronto: Second Story Press, 2011.

Kealey, Linda, and Joan Sangster. *Beyond the Vote: Canadian Women and Politics.* Toronto: University of Toronto Press, 1989.

Kelley, Ninette, and Trebilcock, Michael. *The Making of the Mosaic: A History of Canadian Immigration Policy.* Toronto: University of Toronto Press, 1998.

Knowles, Valerie. *A Biography of Cairine Wilson: First Person, Canada's First Woman Senator.* Toronto: Dundurn Press, 1988.

———. *Strangers at Our Gates: Canadian immigration and immigration policy, 1540-1997.* Toronto: Dundurn Press, 1997.

Miller, William. *Crossing the Atlantic.* Portland, Oregon: Graphic Arts Books, 2007.

———. *The Great Luxury Liners 1927-1954: A Photographic Record.* New York, New York: Dover Publications, 1981.

Ogilvie, Sarah A. and Miller, Scott. *Refuge Denied: The St. Louis Passengers and the Holocaust.* Madison, Wisconsin: The University of Wisconsin Press, 2006.

Public Affairs Nova Scotia. *The Pier 21 Story 1924-1971.* Halifax, 1978.

Thomas, Gordon, and Max Morgan-Witts. *Voyage of the Damned.* New York, New York: Skyhorse Publishing, 2010.

Tulchinsky, Gerald. *Immigration to Canada: Historical Perspectives.* Toronto: Copp Clark Longman, 1994.

Walker, Barrington. *The History of Immigration and Racism in Canada.* Toronto: Canadian Scholars' Press, 2008.

Welldon, Christine. *Pier 21: Listen to My Story.* Halifax: Nimbus Publishing, 2012.

WEBSITES

American Jewish Joint Distribution Committee
www.archives.jdc.org

Canadian Jewish Congress Charities Committee
www.cjccc.ca/en/cjccc-national-archives

Historica Canada Blog: The Canadian Encyclopedia
http://blog.thecanadianencyclopedia.com

Jewish Virtual Library

www.jewishvirtuallibrary.org

The MS *St. Louis* Legacy Project
www.stlouislegacyproject.org

INDEX

Numbers set in italics refer to images.